*Zong!*

WESLEYAN POETRY

# Zong!

## M. NourbeSe Philip

*As told to the author by*

SETAEY ADAMU BOATENG

WESLEYAN UNIVERSITY PRESS

MIDDLETOWN, CONNECTICUT

Published by Wesleyan University Press, Middletown, CT 06459
www.wesleyan.edu/wespress

First Wesleyan paperback 2011

Printed in the United States of America 5 4 3 2

ISBN for the paperback edition: 978-0-8195-7169-4

*Library of Congress Cataloging-in-Publication Data*

Philip, Marlene NourbeSe, 1947–
    Zong! / M. NourbeSe Philip as told to the author by Setaey Adamu Boateng.
      p.  cm.
    ISBN-13: 978-0-8195-6876-2 (alk. paper)
    ISBN-10: 0-8195-6876-7 (alk. paper)
    I. Title.
    PR 9199.3.P456z66 2008
    811'.54—dc22 2007052378

This project is supported in part
by an award from the National
Endowment for the Arts

Wesleyan University Press is a member of the Green Press
Initiative. The paper used in this book meets their minimum
requirement for recycled paper.

*For Lord Yeates,*
*Ti Miss Maam, & the many, many others.*
*Also for Kudakwashe.*

*Though they go mad they shall be sane,*
*Though they sink through the sea they shall rise  again . . .*

DYLAN THOMAS, *And Death Shall Have No Dominion*


*The time is out of joint. O cursèd spite*
*That ever I was born to set it right!*

SHAKESPEARE, *Hamlet*

# Contents

# *Acknowledgments*

A work like *Zong!*, although apparently authored by one person, only comes into being and to fruition with the assistance and support of many others. It is with great joy, therefore, I embrace this opportunity to recognize, acknowledge, and thank the many individuals who have, in one way or another, walked with, or helped, me along the seven-year journey that was the making of *Zong!* My deepest appeciation and thanks to all of them.

More specificically, I would like to thank Paul Chamberlain who has offered continued and generous support over the years, without which this work would not have been possible. He has been particularly helpful in computer matters, and his contribution to the conceptualization of the cover has been invaluable.

I first found reference to the Zong incident in James Walvin's *Black Ivory,* published in 1990. This was the inspiration for *Zong!* Diane Roberts recognized the worth of *Zong!* from its inception, and her support has been steadfast. Ian Baucom very kindly shared his archival research on the Zong massacre with me. Suzanna Tammimen's interest in, and support of, my work, as well as her patience over the years I have been working on *Zong!*, have been been indispensable to the completion of the work. Cristanne Miller has always brought an informed and critical eye to my work; she offered sound advice on the manuscript at a time when it was greatly needed. Sue Houchins offered a forum for me to read from and talk about *Zong!* Her engagement with the formal issues of *Zong!* in conversation with me has helped, over the years, to clarify the theoretical foundations of *Zong!* Tonya Foster generously read the manuscript and offered skilled and helpful suggestions. Robin Pacific's long-standing support of my work has been significant. Her comments on, and responses to, the manuscript have been invaluable. Joss McLennan's ideas and graphic skills were vital to the final resolution of the cover image. Marc Walker generously let me have the use of his farm at various times so that I could work on the manuscript. Hardie Philip-Chamberlain provided invaluable advice on graphics and design issues particularly with respect to the cover design. Hesper Philip-

Chamberlain's responses to *Zong!* have been extremely helpful in clarifying many of my ideas around the work. Bruce King has always kept it real. Kofi Anyidoho guided and assisted me in obtaining spiritual permission for this work. Rainos Mutamba generously mined the text to find words and expressions from the Shona language. The Grip Group, including Natalie, Kike and Avril, provided a cultrual framework and foundation that allowed me greater insight into the nature of the work that is *Zong!* Margaret Christakos reminded me of my presence and through her pathbreaking series, *Influency*, provided me a venue for a critical response to *Zong!* Brent Edwards' and Pat Saunders' critical interest in *Zong!* and support of my work have been significant contributions to the process of writing this work. One does not often thank an author for his or her work, but Modupe Oduyoye's *Yoruba's Names* was vital to my understanding Yoruba and helped me to construct many of the phrases and names that float through the text.

I would also like to thank the Canada Council, the Ontario Arts Council, The Chalmers Fellowship Foundation, the Rockefeller Foundation (Bellagio Residency), for their support. Over the years the following journals have published excerpts from *Zong!*: *Fracture, boundary 2, Mangrove, Hambone,* and *The Capilano Review*.

Finally, I thank the Ancestors for bestowing the responsibility of this work on me. Àse.

*The sea was not a mask.*

WALLACE STEVENS

# Zong! #1

w   w   w                w                    a   wa

     w           a               w a          t

er                wa                              s

   our                          wa

te   r gg                    g           g        go

  o           oo                goo                    d

  waa                          wa wa

w w waa

  ter                      o        oh

on              o                  ne            w one

   w o n                    d d d

  ey                  d            a

dey         a   ah              ay

  s                one                    day s

  wa                wa

---

w w w w  w                                        a

w  wa                          wa                            t

        er                              wa                        te

r                                              wat

        er                                          wa    ter

        of                          w

                ant

_____

Aba  Chimanga  Naeema  Oba  Eshe

*Zong! #2*

                    the throw in  circumstance

      the weight in want

             in sustenance

   for underwriters

             the loss

   the order in destroy

             the that fact

             the it was

             the were

negroes

             the after rains

---

*Zong! #3*

           the some of negroes

                        over

       board

       the rest in lives

                        drowned

       exist did not

                        in themselves

       preservation

                        obliged

frenzy

thirst for forty others

                        etc

---

Nobini  Zesiro  Yaa  Issa  Kambuji

*Zong! #4*

                                  this is

            not was

                                        or

                            should be

             this be

                                  not

          should be

                                  this

            should

                                not

              be

  is

---

Lipapwiche Aziza Chipo Dada Nomsa

*Zong! #5*

of

water

rains &

dead

the more

of

the more

of

negroes

of

water

&

weeks

(three less than)

rains

&

water

(three butts good)

of

sea and

perils

of water

(one day)

water —

*day one . . .*

of months

of

weeks

of

days

of

sustenance

lying

dead

---

Mwita  Muhammad  Mulogo  Becktemba  Hadiya

of

days

of

sour water

enemies &

want

of

died

(seven out of seventeen)

of

good

(the more of)

of

(eighteen instead of six)

dead

of rains

(eleven days)

of

weeks

(thirty not three)

---

Odusanya  Mxali  Ogunba

                    of

                                        water

                                            *day one . . .*

for sustenance

                                            water

                                                *day*

*one . . .*

one day's

                                            water

                                                *day*

*one . . .*

sour

                                            water

                                                *day*

*one . . .*

three butts good

                    of voyage

                    (a month's)

of necessity

sufficient

and

last

the more

of

exist

want &

less than

of did not

&

the more of

of suffered

did not

exist

sustenance

water &

want

of

---

Ngolinda Amina Kiambu Ngunda Nobanzi

dead

the more of

of negroes

the more

of

instead

of

## *Zong! #6*

question therefore

the age

eighteen weeks

and calm

but it is said . . .

— from the maps

and

contradicted

by the evidence . . .

question

therefore

the age

*Zong! #7*

first:

the when

the which

the who

the were

the throwing

overboard

the be

come apprehended

exist did not

Wemusa  Ilesanmi  Nayo  Odai

*Zong! #8*

        the good of overboard

        justified a throwing

                of property

                  fellow

creatures

      become

             our portion

              of

             mortality

       provision

            a bad market

negroes

                    want

       for dying

*Zong! #9*

                                                              slaves

                                                      to the order in

                destroyed

                                            the circumstance in

                fact

                                                the property in

                subject

                                                    the subject in

                creature

                                                        the loss in

                underwriter

                                                    to the fellow in

                negro

                                                    the sustenance

                in want

                                    the arrived

in vessel

                                    the weight

in provisions

                                    the suffered in

 die

                                    the me in

become

*Zong! #10*

should have

was reduced

retarded

rendered

could

found

given

sailed

bring to

occurred

throwing

arose

to be

was

were

passed

justify

appeared

authorize

made might

---

Oluseyi  Fatoki  Abifarin  Soremekun  Kwakou

*Zong! #11*

suppose the law

is

not

does

not

would

not

be

not


suppose the law not

— a crime

suppose the law a loss

suppose the law

suppose

## Zong! #12

it

is said

has been decided

was justified

appeared impossible

is not necessary

is another ground

need not be proved

it

was a throwing overboard

it

is a particular circumstance

need not be proved

is another ground

is not necessary

appeared impossible

Oni  Sanura  Mashama  Sigolwide  Shamfa

was justified

has been decided

is said

it

was

---

Mhonum Ajike Odunmbaku Maizah Oku Lizige

*Zong! #13*

the rest of

the more of

the half of

out of

fifty of

instead of

negroes

the necessity of

*Zong! #14*

the truth was

        the ship sailed

        the rains came

        the loss arose

                the truth is

the ship sailed

the rains came

the loss arose

                the negroes is

the truth was

Nkrumah  Ato  Nobanzi  Oduneye  Opa  Fagbulu

*Zong! #15*

defend the dead

           weight of circumstance

ground

      to usual &

          etc

          where the ratio of just

in less than

        is necessary

            to murder

the subject in property

the save in underwriter

          where etc tunes justice

          and the *ratio* of murder

          is

          the usual in occurred

---

Akilah  Falope  Ouma  Weke  Jubade

the just in ration

the suffer in loss

defend the dead

the weight

in

circumstance

ached in necessary

the ration in just

age the act in the *ave* to justice

---

## *Zong! #16*

should they have

found being

        sufficient

        a necessity

(portion that question)

should they have

        found the justify

for exist

        a rule for new

        the policy within the loss

(portion that question etc)

should they —

might they have

        found

---

Nompumelelo  Okulaja  Ekisola  Abike  Arike

the of and during & wherefore

the preserving

the insurance of water

the within loss

the terms of exist

a negro of wit

should they have found

water

&

being

sufficient

## *Zong! #17*

there was

    the this

    the that

    the frenzy

        leaky seas &

          casks

          negroes of no belonging

on board

no rest

    came the rains

    came the negroes

    came the perils

    came the owners

        master and mariners

---

Adunni  Akanni  Akanbi  Alade  Alayande

                                        the this

                                        the that

                                        the frenzy

came the insurance of water

water of good only


came water sufficient

that was truth

& seas of mortality

                                question the now

                    the this

                    the that

                    the frenzy




not unwisely



Ayoka  Faluyi  Owolabi  Oni  Sowole  Mudiwa

*Zong! #18*

                                    means

                    truth

                    means           overboard

                                    means

                    sufficient

                    means           support

                                    means

                    foul

                    means           three butts

                                    means

                    necessity

                    means           provisions

                                    means

                    perils

Toyin  Sipho  Adelabu  Lisabi  Fayemi  Eki

means                    evidence

                         means

mortality

means                    policy

                         means

voyage

means                    market

                         means

slaves

means                    more

                         means

dead

means                    want

water

means                    water

*Zong! #19*

drowned the law

        their thirst &

        the evidence

        obliged the frenzy

in themselves

in the sea

        ground the justify

        in the necessity of

when

who &

which

Gbolade  Ololade  Mapfumo  Ngunda  Dayo

there is no evidence

in the against of winds

the consequence of currents

or

the apprehension of rains

the certain of value

or

the value in certain


against the rest in preservation

the save in residue

negroes exist

for the throwing

*Zong! #20*

this necessity of loss

this quantity of not

perils underwriters

insurers

of

the throw in circumstance

the instance in attempt

the attempt in voyage

the may in become

in

the between of day

a sea of negroes

drowned

live

in the thirst

Oriyome Fasuyi Olaifa Ekua Bobo Kobie

for

otherwise

the sure of verdict

in the want of action

preserve the soon in afterwards

the time in africa

to jamaica

now the question

falls

upon

enemies

*Zong! #21*

                              is being is

              or

      should

                        is is

          is

          be

      being

              or

      been

                        is was

          is

            should be

                    or

          have been

                  is there

_____

Ayodele  Oluwa  Oje  Olayinka  Motayo  Babatunde

was

should

was not

should be

or

have been

is there is

or

being

there

is was

is is

should

and

have been

there is

was

there

Ogunade Omotayo Yewande Abibola Sonubi Abeke

*Zong! #22*

lives own their facts

     of spent lives

      murder

      market

     misfortunes

        &

      policy

lying dead

under seas

    facts own their lives

in circumstance

    &

happening

       in trial &

declaration

     in the absolute

of rule

   &

lord

in the absolute

      of water

---

Muru  Kakra  Kolawole  Kibibi  Olabisi  Usi

*Zong! #23*

was

    the weight in being

    the same in rains

    the ration in loss

    the proved in fact

    the within in is

    the sufficient in indictment

    the might have in existed

is

    the evidence in negroes

*Zong! #24*

evidence

    is
  sustenance
    is
  support
    is
  the law

the ship

    is
  the captain
    is
  the crew

perils

    is
  the trial
    is
  the rains
    is
  the seas
    is
  the currents

jamaica

    is
  tobago
    is
  islands

the case

    is

      murder

---

```
                    is
                 justice

    africa

                 is
              the ground
                 is
              negroes

                                evidence is
                                  sustenance is
                                      support is
                                     the law is
                                     the ship is
                                   the captain is
                                     the crew is
                                       perils is
                                     the trial is
                                     the rains is
                                      the seas is
                                     currents is
                                      jamaica is
                                      tobago is
                                      islands is
                                     the case is
                                      murder is
                                      justice is
                                   the ground is
                                      africa is


                                          negroes


                  was
```

---

Oluyemi  Esugbayi  Adubifa  Ogunlesi  Akua

*Zong! #25*

justify the could

         the captain &

         the crew

         the authorize

in captain

crew &

could

                could authorize justify

                          captain

      &

        crew

                          the

                          could

or justify authorize

           could

           captain & crew

                    authorize

---

Bomani  Yahya  Modupe  Jibowu  Fayola

the crew

the captain &

the could

                                        the justify

                                                    in

captain

                                                could &

                                                crew

                                    in authorize


justify

            the could

            the captain &

            the crew

                        justify the authorize

                            the could

*Zong! #26*

was the cause was the remedy was the record was the argument
was the delay was the evidence was overboard was the not was the
cause was the was was the need was the case was the perils was the
want was the particular circumstance was the seas was the costs
was the could was the would was the policy was the loss was the
vessel was the rains was the order was the that was the this was the
necessity was the mistake was the captain was the crew was the
result was justified was the voyage was the water was the maps
was the weeks was the winds was the calms was the captain was
the seas was the rains was uncommon was the declaration was the
apprehension was the voyage was destroyed was thrown was the
question was the therefore was the this was the that was the
negroes was the cause

Omolara  Chimaneya  Adekemi  Oke  Mowunmi  Iliola

# DICTA

*Zong! #*

seas without
        insurers
        owners
        perils
        islands
        africa

                owners without

africa
seas
insurers
islands
perils

      africa without

          perils
          seas
          insurers
          islands
          owners

———————————————————

*Zong! #*

clear the law

of

order

cause

delay

of question

&

opinion

of the etc of negroes

the no is proved

---

*Zong!* #

150sixtyfortytwoandahalfeleventhreesevenfiftythirtyseveneighteenseventeenonesix
               weeks
               months
               weeks
               days
               months
               days
               weeks
               months
               weeks
               months
               weeks
                         negroes


                         was the bad made measure

*Zong! #*

                                                        islands
                                                            first
                                                            any
                                                            many
                                                            eighteen
                                                            other
                                                            three
                                                            particular

                                        currents
                                any
                                many
                            eighteen
                                other
                                three
                        particular
                                first
winds
        many
        eighteen
        other
        three
        particular
        first
        any

                                                weeks
                            eighteen
                                other
                                three
                        particular
                                first
                                any
                                many

                    misfortunes
        other
        three
    particular
        first
        any
        many
    eighteen
                                            mistake s
                                                three
                                                particular
                                                first
                                                any
                                                many
                                                eighteen
                                                other
                        calms
            particular
            first
            any
            many
            eighteen
            other
            three

                                        negroes
                                            first
                                            any
                                            many
                                            eighteen
                                            other
                                            three
                                            particular
                                            contrary

*Zong! #*

                                        underwriters

                                                    of

                                                perils
                                                necessity

    &

                                                    mortality

                    of

                        soon

                        only        &

                        afterwards

                                        of was and

            not &

                                                        them was

    slaves

            not

                        evidence

                    _____

*Zong! #*

uncommon case

great weight                                                    new trial

great weight

new trial                                                    uncommon case

new trial

uncommon case                                                    great weight

uncommon weight

great trial                                                    new case

great trial

new case                                                    uncommon weight

---

new case

uncommon weight                                          great trial

uncommon trial

great case                                          new weight

great case

new weight                                          uncommon trial

new weight

uncommon trial                                          great case

*Sal*

*Non enim erat tunc.*
*There was no then.*

ST. AUGUSTINE

water parts

the *oba* sobs

there is

creed there is

fate there is

oh                                    oh oracle

there are

oh oh

ashes

over

*ifá*

*ifá*

*ifá i*

*fá*

fa

fa                                    fall

ing over

&

over the crew

touching there                        is fate

there is

creed

there is

oh

oh

the *oba* sobs

again *ifá*                           *ifá ifá i*

*fá* over          and over

the seven

seas                                  *ora*

in this time                          *ora*

within          *ora ora*                    time within

loss                                    *ora pro*

          this is but                         an o

               ration time                         sands

the loss within                         how many

          days how long                              where being is

thirst & thirst                    be being she                         falls

          fortunes over                         board rub

                    and rob her

now i lose               count i am                         lord

          of loss visions               over and                         over the *o*

*ba* sobs               from there to                    here bring them

                    no provisions                         from is

          to wa                              s sow

               the seas

                    with she

                         negroes ma

     n negroes murder                                   my lord

          my liege lord

                    my *deus*

               my us

          my we                              my fate

my god                              sun

          der crew

     from captain                         own

               from slave

                         under

from

                         writer from

          mortality

                    *mort*

*le mort le*

        *mort le p tit mort*

               scent of mortality

     she

      falls

*ifáifáifá*

    falling                    to

          port

            over

      &
     over

       my fortunes

      a sin         you say

*video video vide*       *o* who says i am

       the lord           of loss a rose

i say          a rose

    for ruth        and for t

      ruth sup        pose truth

        then find

ing         a way

    found        a port

       a rule ought

     evidence

         suppose then t

   ruth      a rose

    over

        &

over

       with you

    she f          alls falling

found                                        a rose fou

                    nd africa                                    un

        der water

                                proved

justice                    danger

        ous                            the law

        a crime she

                    died es                        es es

        oh                            es

        oh oh                es es            oh

            es            s            o

                s                s            o

                s                    s

                        o  s

                    os

    os

            *os*

                            bone

        us us *os*

            save us *os*

        salve                                    & save

                            our souls tone

& turn the bo            nes

                        &

        salve                    our souls u

    s souls

            bo                            ne souls

                salve the slav

        e *salve* to

sin *salve*                slave *salve*

and *ave*                                    *ave*

    the rat the                                    rat *ave*

           ah we                              cut cut

cut the                    cost and serve              where s the cat

    the yam                    no meat                    trim

the loss                                    payment

      you say what                              for where s

           the cat got

       the rat could

   the crime out                              out

cut the ear                              be absolute do

    you hear

       the lute sound

  to raise                              the dead

    the died

     i hear

       *ave* bell s

  ring                              out

     dear ruth

    this is                    a tale told

     cold a yarn

a story dear                    dear ruth i

   woo time                              and you do

     i have y our

ear                              there were aster s

   at tea time éclairs                              & you

     are my liege

   lord of nig                    nig &

     nog                    my *doge*

         there are

stars in

*sidera*

as there is

*ratio*

in rations

but why ruth

do the stars                shine                    if only

murder made us            you  were by my side

*os*

*os*                                    *os*

bo                                        ne men

misfortunes

very  new

and                                                    we map

uncommon                            the usual

to me            to the vessel            winds & currents

we ground            upon

i pen this

to you

when i am                                        her

able                                            paps her

dugs                            her

teats

leak in necessity                    there

was sin a good                        supply of

ply the negroes                        with

toys lure them

visions of l                                    ace for a queen

my queen

there is pus

dire visions

tempt all                night ride                me *dis moi*

        do you

    ruth                might you

and i                    perils

   notwithstanding we

seek the *ratio*           in africa negroes

     too

  *de men*        *dem cam fo mi*

    for  me for

*yo* for *je*

          *pour moi* & *para*

  *mi* flee

the fields      *gun bam*     *bam*

   it was        oh oh

  a falling

          my fate

come to term         & murder

  in lies          grounds justice

the noise     in lives

  a discharge    him touch

   ing might     you and i

         ruth

   oh the noise

  nig nig nig     there was

zen in frenzy      & nog

    nag

   nag

 all night

  it is the age of guns

gin                                                                              & rum of

        murder                                              rimed with sin

                                        her sex

            open all                              night rain

                a seam of sin &

to market to market                                tin

                                                        such

                        to trap a fat pig

            a fat nig                                as never be

fore seen

                        lords of reason

        all we were                                a lace cap for my

                and sane men too                                queen

                        sapphire  too

    for my lady                                gold

                *el  son*                                a

                        song                                at vespers

                                she rides

        my nights the                                bell the good ship

                vedic visions no

    gongs                                provisions

                *niger sum nigra*                        *sum ego*

        *sum* i

            am                        yam                ben

am                        am        gin

                        am rum make the mast

        teak men

                who can cure

                                                    me the cur

    drag the seas                        seven  miles

seven                deep

    days

weeks             for *ius*                    sing a song

    months           for us                 of water

      for *os*           in bone

        for bone a deep

    wa                 ter water

    deep bo

ne son            g to cradle

    her where the sun

      sink s

  under                throw them

    the rim       crusts lost       verses

    of sky circe      the seer

      appears

lip s in rictus            there is an art

    to murder

with rant and curse         but the tense

    is all        wrong rum

  rain and more

rum ah         but it s a rum

  tale ruth murder        & rum they sang &

      sang

    &

she negroes      sang

mean        *le sang*

  red verses        groans *de men dem*

    *cam fo mi*

  here &             there

    a line          i

write                                        to
you                                                          of
                              mortality s
        lien on l
ife
                      on the
            ro
      se
                  on
      bo            ne                                        on
ne                      groes
                                          such  drab  necessity
              murder
here we                        re negroes
                                    like  ants
        sow the sea                        *is where*
*we be*                    seed the seas
        with es &                  oh & es                        *os*
                                    &
      us
            our pig got                          with n
got                        our nig too              egroes
                              pai
      n captain  pai                      n
                                    tha
  t hat                                        that hat
                        the rat mi lord
      my plea is negligence                  to her i
            say *te amo*

her name                                           she smiles

will be es                               se to be                    i smile

and i                          am                        fall

am                                                          falling

am *sum*                        into

of all                        murder

am sum                                        am

*ame*                                              if

if

if

if only *ifá*

serve                                                              the *oba*

sobs again

the tea  men                          there was piss *cum*

let s have some                          bile *cum* pus

jam and                          bread

port too

& leaky

teats                                        there was only

bilge wat

er for tea

i argue my case

to you                                                        take

ruth                                        everything

you must hear me                          i say

*cum grano*                        *salis*

with a grain of                          salt there was in

surance again

st sun                          not sin

hum hum            hum him him

& him too

a hero he was        and a negro

we dare

the deed

act the part        he cut

the cards i won the        throw one

deuce        two aces

cut

her

open her

shape        tie her

ripe        toes

round

and firm

the cord        it is

dead she went        over &

under she was

wet put

ashes

on her water s

leak oil        her and bring

her

to me        no god

no i should

cut the cord of this        story

i rest

my case        in negligence my plea

ignorance *ave*        to *àse*

to *ilé ifè*          *salve*

to cain                              to abel too

we need must

meet with the east &

the west kings                    be queens

slaves too

slip lip over              nip the rose              she spin s

in the bud                    once

once

more

falls                              the *oba*

sobs

again                    & again the

tense the time

is all

wrong what will

mend

my mind i cede                    all good

in the span of                    pain

lisp my

longing she falls                    i will

loan                    her

to you ration                    the yam and

the facts pain

cap n pain                    ma ma pat

pat she s done                    for

*rêve* master              *rêve* the she negro

he s done for                    drives me

mad *je rêve je*                    *rêve* him him

him & him                    her

too

din din

dong

*aide moi* i            ration the truth                              the she negro

ruth                                          drives me mad

and the facts

whore they laid her

to rest she died

*lave* the slave            invest in

tin                  in

rum                  in

slaves                        in

negroes serve                        the preserve

the jam            and jamaica

rum i                    remain god s jest

rimed

with sin rest                        master rest we

have the ram                          is it

just or just

us i *rêve* of                        aster s

*éclair s*

and ruth                              such a good

dog pat                              pat nig

nig nig

nog

nag the man

ran the slave                        ran ma

ma *mma ma*                        *mai* bard sing

stir my thirst                        for song a ruse

run ruth run

from me                                        & my sin mea

      sure the ease

               of

          over

      board      all

  fled the lair

            as if

    on wing         how

such a thin

       mite he

        was just

    seven

     *de man him*

*cam*       *fo mi a fez*

  *pon his head* row     row row the raft

    how *orí*

     *orí*    a gin nig

nig nig     *orí oh*    nig

   *omi*    *omi*

  nog &     *omi*

    *oh*    nag

  wa    wa

     ter *j ai*

*soif* she stirs    my    thirst

    an ace and

a deuce it was    pen my nig

   my pig then    they came

    for me *mes*

  *rêves* our aim    to rid the good

   ship of dying    & death

of them

the way　　　　　　　　　　　　　　　　　　broad & wide

　　as it was　　　　　　　　　long i won

her fair　　　　　　the pig got

　　got to the east　　　　　　　　　& west over

the seas to sin　　　　　　am i

　　a man　　　　　　　of wit

ruth i hear　　　　you say

　　some see　　　　the dove

on wing　　　the red　　　　cove

　　*le sang le*　　　　　　*sing le* song

　　*le son el*　　　　*son* oh god no　　　hug

　　and tug *mai* she　　　　ran *ma* he

ran *ma ba*　　　　*ba iya* they　　　ran

　　the cat got gut

are we thugs　　　all gut　　　her

*no no no*　　　*run*　　　*run if you hear*

　　*dogs hide the gods*

　　　*are gone done*

　*for hey*

　　*hola*

　　　　run round &

　　round　　　sound of dog

　of song there is　　pus it rains

sin sip sup　　　and doze a dose

　of the clap

　　suppose the hat

　　　rode the rat round

and round　　　　the fins

　herd them　　　the crew does

75

my bid  no sound                                              bell song lure

              her dong she                                                    dives dong

        to the rim over                    with you and                                        under she f

              alls falling                                    appears under

                          water found                                    africa

              a rose                                    round

        and round the hat                                          the rat

                          the rot oh                          the rot we

              sort them new

                                              rules state the test

                          man for men

              & for t                              ruth ask rome

              fist to the head mis                          fortunes tune pain

                          turn &

        turn a                                          round the globe

                    bill the bell

                                              & bell

              the cat she was                                    torn we sear

                          & singe the rose

              of afric a mole

        on her nape a bill                                          of sale flap

                                    flap

              in the wind the sail            seal

        the sale sad

                                        sail s night            falls so far

              to afric & the dog

                                              star

*Ventus*

*The poet is the detective and the detective a poet.*

THOMAS MORE

                                              sh h
                                      not so
loud did nt the                               bell ring oh
                          oh my
            ass
                  hot                                     apes
      all sing                                                sing
            they sang *le*                      *sang el*
                        song *le*                    song sing
            again                                            my goat bag of
                              palm wine
                  dance                    dance they sing my
                        ass
      lips gape oh                    oh sad tune
                  sing again                    they groan not
                        so loud
      *when did we decide*              desire              *le sang*
                              pain              oh oh
            they ma ma *mai*
                                    with no
      notes                    tears they
                  sit *moi je*                          am they
            lie
over                          them
            the sun sow                    the seven
                        seas
            with              *aves*                          of am
            & ash sing                          him *oba*
                  him
                              *ask tiki tiki*
      *fo me*                    the ship                    heaves
            sing i say                          to
                              &
                  fro                    groans
the *oba* sobs again              the din of my
            own my very
                              own dying
                  negroes a pint
      of gin the candle                          flame s and a hey
                              hey ho once                    an
                  am
            died              dead

in its      sconce

    he had an

      ace       dear ruth

can a tale be

     told

       ever

i       held      a  sequence

      of

     queens

one

king

      *tsuh chu*

i

    come

     from

the north     the

    dales      land

    of mist

of hoar      frost

     dear     ruth

there is

us

     &

   *os*

there is bone      *why does the*

   a secret race under     *shin bone shine so ruth*

writers     lives  of writ s

& rent s      cede

   the truth

    to the right

to be sure

    this is      but

    an oration

a tale

*there is ruse*    old

*in insure*      as

   sin    is

   new

    circe

the crone

    lips

a gape

     sings

a

*did we decide*     tune

it rains writ s

piss     & bile

to the right     ran pus

the truth

& sin to be sure

tears

rum

&

why are we here

&

where are

we    *we act the part but ration*

dance    *the facts*

dance

dance

i say

they sit

they lie

i

captain    their pain

wind

strum s    the air

he strums    the oud

the ship

cradles    our longing

our    lust    our

loss    all

that is    old    in this

new    age

the time    the

date of

sin

clara

that tune again

the air    it calms me

but    then

the    drum s

oh

the    drum s

all night    they pray

for    death

shout    *lisa*

*lisa*

dear

ruth    if

a tale

*ora*

*ora*    be    told

*ora*            cold

    pray for me

       & heave         men

heave               and

       pass

    the peas       ignore

     the pleas            *omi*

           *omi*

       *l eau*

*l eau*

       water      clair

        the

     sound

   of the oud

       rouse s me

    the

   air     is

    danger     ous

    with

       drum

sound

   i hear              them

   words            strange

    to my

   ear      the *oba* smiles

    he has       *owó*

    guineas

   *cedis*    too     i have

    guinea    negroes

     they

  shed

    tears

   for     *ifá*

  *ósun*

    &

  *ógún*

         for

   *efun*

     for

    *èsú*

   ask for

  *ame*

   from

*olú*

  his eyes

rage

                would
        bring                                        mi
                me                          run
to                      death                from
        if              field              de
                he              man in de          hat
        could                          dem
        she died            cam fo                  mi
on                      a tide      him
        of red                      fun fun
    up river                                me ode
                                    where
        we dare                      efun
                    our *mortality by the*
        desire      *tail*
at          dawn        *on the run*
        if          if              if only
            *ifa*
    was                 yak yak
        yak yak
    yam             pleas
            my
        own
    she
                        negro
                            the
            wonder
of          it
            a               dower
    gift            for
        you
                    grain
    in      the
        field               sun
            overhead
        in
                        your
                hair
        gold            as
                    corn *first*

*act  third scene*
            circe argues with eve
    about eden                  on the eve
                    of murder
        rome mourns
    her

83

misfortune
        her
    *mort*
          her
    *p tit mort*
           turns
        from
                ruins
            of forts
      and        fortunes
              to
        found
              a
         city
            on
              death
         on
                  murder circe
to eve
              there is no             *writ in sand*
        evidence of eden            *lives rent*
in eve eve                 to circe    *lives*
                i am
    circe                    the seer
sings a      tune a sad tune
                with no no
    tes *moi*        *je* am he
              am she
      am at last            *omi* water
  *l eau*              *l eau*
        *il doge* wears
  a hat it is          red as is
    his cape up
         and
     down up            and
          down the wind
        rose bail
   bail & bail
     water water the
wind            rose is wet
               no
        help *omi*
   *omi omi* under
     wind & up
             wind  we sail
     with every

wind create a cat s        cradle on

     the sea sing *te*

           *deum s* the bells

the bells ding ding

           and dong over

     the water done done            deed done died

       done dead

there is fresh            fish no water

     rush rush feet

       guns run red

         run dear lisa

dave ask s this            is but

     an oration he            ask s that i

       these words

come that i        write from his lips

     though my hand            shapes why

       are we here dear

         clair i

     write      this

       for

      sam       who

        is

       by

      my

         side

       there was

     ague         on

       board

        pus

    too dear eve

piet says       he longs

         dear eva

       davenport      i fear

      the news         is

       not      good

     today at ten

at four        at

   six        &        at

     seven       my hand

    writes

   we seal      the deal      the sale      of

       negroes

    on      board      the

   sail

    slap     slap        in

the                      wind

some

come          from              the fens

others     from the     dales

and               the         far

off               of

africa i want           a

hat      of

fur            for        you

ruth         shine         the

negroes     for sale           the wig

w ogs         the nig

nogs        get

the      tongs     the

irons     hot

hot        sing

sing     a            son

g     of

sin     such

a

din

such

a           ding

ding     dong

sing

he     sang

*ba ba*

*iya*

*mma*

ma ma

the

raw

sea             some

rush

nothing       but

a raft

my once       queen

now slave        there be

no free      on

board

under

writers

tire

of writs

writ fine

with sin

m lord
the
questions                    can
we
sin          within
the          law
can                    the
law
sin sail
west
then east
east
then west
in              the hang
of
*when did we*            rope                              there
*decide*                                                        exists
*hofi*
a span
of pain
such
that
the
poet                                    of
the                    trope
that is
troy          can
not                          own
but          there                    is
property          i
say
in
pope
in
troy          in
rome
in
negro
in
guns
bam bam
our                                        eyes
skim          the sea                              for
bodie s for          the law          in                    *ius* in
us                    in
*os* in                    bone how
many

did            you did
        i how
            many did                         we
                            sir what
                    say you                 no a
            queen
                    once            now
            my
whore                    to the  crew
                                            too
            are we but                  bone
                            men
                                    with
                            out
                    souls
                        seed        to
                the      ever    in
                            us              the
    story                              waits
                            can      not      be
            told
                                the *oba*
        sobs
            again *act*
                            *scene* m lord
            says the law
                                    is never
wrong can                        never
            sin the negro
            asks                            that i
            write
                            a
                most            un
    common negro he                      hopes to re
                        gain africa
            one day his                        na
me is *wale*                          he wants that
                    they should wait
            for him my eyes                      rest where the sea
    is                  a              line a  lace cap
                    & red cape
            with fur
            for my                      once
                    & nonce queen
                                            my she
negro make the mast

teak men                    for

flag nation

king & pope seek            the eyes hold        the hands tie

the feet

the cut

ran                    from eye to

ear dear miss

circe hans writes

i ask                for your hand peter

piet        writes to miss clara                ted

to miss tara            asif to

um                jon roy

& ned tom tim

alf & jim

mike & dave

my crew

mates

all

a mob rum gin                beer &

cider

there was                grin

and gin        *a fortune in forts ahena*

gin and        *adwoa & danger*

grin round & round            *fifi*

the globe                we sail the sun s

orb to                lead us  if

we can only gain                the is

land circe

the seer

pants

waits

tempts with

oracles

a trail of feet

in the sand

leads

to the water            a

most un

common negro *you*

*take*

*pen you*

*write*

*to*

*my sade*        i

play        a ruse        on

him

a trail of
lies
lead to                              my truth tame
the rage                                    dance
                                                 dance
                    i say *act*
*scene* my
part is                        set
         bring me my
    cape my
                    mask my past
                                    clap
                   clap i
         play                captain
              pope                        &
         king i                    play
                        god
              but
                                    he s got the clap clap
                   men clap too
limp
                             to
         tup her do
                                        you take
                    this negro to be
                             y our slave we
         make good
                                             time the wind
                                        is
                             with us
                                  a    se
                   cret race
                                  we
                        differ
                             are
we
                                        mad
                   or
    merely                        men
              without
    maps                        in        an
                             age
              where
truth                        is rare        and
                        we                    *dem cam fo me*
              dare              *de man in de fez*

90

not         his

eyes        a

*his eyes*        secret

*rage*        race

*adzo*        with

*ama*        a        taste

*esi*        for the she

negro & port pus

& ague they

faint sam        has a dose

of the clap too

and fine lace

for his

lady flip her over        & over

board was

a red dawn

they

were        drawn

down

ward

a re

ed        for        air

d

own

do

wn        dow

n        down

water

drag s

against

the grain

no        air

in        vain

then        they

were

ever

gone

divers        pour

*les*        *âmes*

nig        *les*        souls

nig

nog

nag

nag

pleas

air

fresh
air          *omi*
water        the
hag
circe        makes
a        ring
of        stones                    in the sand
her o
mens have no
song
or
sound they                    sing
of
the
pact
of                    pain
be
tween
cain                    & abel
bet
ween
ma
n
&
g                    od they
sing they
dance i miss
the                    city
ruth
*tro odu*
a pint                    *fo*
of                    *me*
beer            *omi se o ore*
you
say                    ma
rk them
yes
let s
their        eyes
stare
such
fine    linen
my    lord
for        you
for            her
bod y    not
for    me

for                her
                                        my
        nonce
        my
once

                    queen
            the              t
ruth
                        in
                    her
            eyes
                    circe
            waits
            lips                        hang
                    make s
                fun
            of
                            eros
            of              us
                    &
        *ius*    makes
            pigs    of
                us
                    bail
    bail
            if
        you re      able
            or      abel
                dan
            and
    sam
            saw
        it
                    we
all
    saw it                          why does the *oba* sob
        all day
    it          ran
        rain
    i
        long
            for      man
    y              man
        negroes
            she
                            negroes
                    too

                                        for                    sale
                                    *fon*
                                *ewe*
                    *san*
            *lua*                                    *& rada*
                        pla
                    y            man
                            p
                        lay
        it s
                    an
            old
                        tune
        strum
                it
            for
                    me
            all
                            day
                a
                    tub
                of        wa
                        ter
                    to
            share
                let us
        claire
                just
us                  just
            us
        &
            *ius*
        slip
            y our        lips
    over            these
        words
            an other        man
                writes
            in                    the
                        sack
                of
            troy        the
                rage
            of            men
                    lives
                the
            poet

writes

waits

for

the

past

to

part

for     the

red     sea

for                              the

nation

*inter*                *pares*

for        the

city

of

g                              od

with          no

go              d                    spare

us

*pater*          *mon*

*père*

the                              truth

ru                    th cl

air ro

se

ev

e e                          va

cla                              ra sa

ra

co                              ra ma

ry etc

all

wait

& wait

and

wait

& wait

for                    a

ship

to

bring

their

men

to

them          *dem cam fo mi*

scent

of

cunt        &

      ruth       he

    dove     she

      dove

       they

     dove        *omi*

*omi*         *omi*

   oh       my go

    d       they

were    go       ne

   the    ne

   groes

    ever     claire

the       dove     cote

where

the       doves

    nest

   row

row    slaves

   save     the

boat    the

     slaves      pig

   got       got      nig

got      got     in

eden s      air

   deer     and

    lion    cub

   will    lie

    one

with

    the

     other      we

     will      sail

   to      the

end    to       eden

   my    doe

     eye d    queen

      once

    &

  nonce

   now

slave

   ruth

    read

this    sire

   i will      rise

                              rise
                    say              the
            *aves*          *&*
            *salves*                the
                    *meas*
                         *&*
        *culpa s*                          pray
                *pour*
        *les âmes*                              for
                            *les*
                        souls
                    of          the
                                    slaves
        &
                        my own
            tie the
                            ram              *agbo master*
                to the              *agbo for*
            mast          men        *ori*
*mon*
                *âme*              *mon*
                    *âme*              mo
                    name
                                    my
                        name
                            we
        sailed
                                    up
                                the
            cunt                    of
        africa                  to
                                    found
                                an
                    out
            caste
                        race
                    can t
        you                      add
                a                      market
                    waits
                    it          fans      the
                        deed s                alms
                    for
            the          poet          of
    troy
                for

97

the poet                    of
        the        past
            it                    parts
into                    then
            &
        now come
            strum                    the
                lute
        a                    song
            for                    clara
    &                    clair            for
        ruth                    and
sara
                        how many
        did            i did
            you did            we
            they            drum
                a
    rude                                    sound how
                        they dance
                always
            seek                    the
                eyes
        the bard            mourns
            piss                                    bile
                                shit
            and                    dung my
                liege            lord                    of
                life of                    death
                            *aide*
                    *moi ai*
                    *de mo*            *i aid*
        *e m*                    *oi*            *thro*
            dance            *odu*
                dance        *fo*        *me*
        dance                    *omi*        *se*        *o ore*
                    *j ai faim*                    *ma*
    rk them                    mark them mark        dem *j ai*
            *faim j*
        *ai soif*                    dindin
                dong            dung
        don        din
            din        don        don                    ding
ding
        dong                                    done

*Ratio*

*No one bears witness for the witness.*

PAUL CÉLAN

shave me

now de        cant

the port    do you

        hear    him

pass        the peas

pleas

all round        slap

her slap slap

        of

sail there    was only

when not    if & ashes

to   seal this act    of

skin of sin

of what a    deal my elation

ran

riot    my    seal

on    a   deal

well    done

i    see you   kate

clad

in    fur   the

ring    how   many

carats

you ask

forty    i

say ben   the lad  lay   dead

*mi*    *omo*

   *mi*   *omo* dear

ruth this   is a

tale   told

cold  an   old

tale   one

note a   song an

aria   for  clair

for  kate  for   clara

                    &                  ruth

            etc                                but

                 seal  the

sale                  &         hear

   my             tale

                  told

      cold                    sh h

                  the

        clarion

sounds                 for

  me           is it              a detail

              man

                  he was

             of

   mien        hard

&         cold

 the                  sobs oh

  the sobs       sam         was first

    mate the

                  *oba*

   sobs      again

        *omi se*

o      *ore*      over     and    over

        again     this

   creed of           greed

       is

new      it      seeds      the

  the

   sea s       feeds     the

    lust      for

     tin     for

gold

   comes       to  rest

     in   rest

   rest  my   pet

      my  she

    negro

    how do

we            parse

the deed is                              it one

or

many how

do                              we

praise                              the

dead                    a                    job

well done                    the

captain                              says                    the

pain the

pain *le pain le*          *pain el pan*                              pant

pant &          paint

it do                    i

have your

ear i rave i

rave i *rêve*                              *je*

*rêve mes*

*rêves*

*les*                    *rêves* in                    the e

den

of                    our gar

den you                              and i ruth will

have stag s                              boar s &

deer                              carp in

the river doves

there

will be dogs                    fish                                        &

grouse                    owls &

tit s pea hen s too no                    pigs he

negroes                    &she

negroes *je*

*rêve je*

*rêve* pain has                    *rêves*

a lease on *mes*

erase                    this erase

me*aveaveave*

slave save                    the

*ave s* save the                    *salve s* the *vale s*

too but not                              the

slaves                    bilge

water

with scum

for tea bite  him *him*

*big man him fun*

*fun*  hey hey

hey here's

an oar row  row she rode

the roar the  awe of raw

water *ba*  *ba iya*

*ifá* one  day a clear

day it  was no

mist in  the vale the dray

cart  the  hay clipclopclip

clop you and i  rush

& mud  huts we

will

rush the huts *let*

*we*  *rush de cap n de*

*crew* thud hold him

lead her big

with big

*dat hat de fun*

*fun*  *man* this

is a sin we will  rush the

captain the  crew

you ask

me  i beg

dem fo  *ayo fo sade*

*fo*

*mi omo fo mi*

*pic kin* the sun s

rays hot the gibes held  him led her the  negro rat

a tat rat a  tat rat a

tat tat dan jon &  will my  crew

mates good men  all who

ever holds

the globe spills  the gore

dan is just  a lad *sit dem*

*seh dem*  eat beef  dem

*have beer dem*  *lav a*

*lav a* the  shit the piss

       & bile much         ho

          hum dear      clair we

            sat to

    tea oily

beef             and beer even

   port some jam         & spuds we

     ate how do         we praise

murder i

        grieve my

  fate my soul my      late soul my

    fortunes the loss      of every thing every

truth my action         a

   sin no man    can the awe       of

    one tear in    a sea against the

      hard       reef of rea

son i

      war with my

  self *iya*       *ba ba am beg you*

    *do ebo fo mi* they

  use their limb s

        as oar s *je*

  *rêve je*       *rêve* is

    it was it     real master sir

   *me i*     *beg you you*     *write fo mi you*

    *say ayo dem*     *cam fo mi in*

    *de field me run*

*run rat*       *a tat tat*     if

  *ífa* if *ífa* if

        only *ífa oh*

   *les rêves* erase

me       clip clop clip

  clop we         act the part

   most apt    for murder i play

    my part my past

my robe & gold       orb *el orbe*

    *de oro* my mask

  if jim        and if

   jam am jam

    am jam *lave*

l eau lave l eau                                            lave l eau je

                        me lave je

            me lave de sin                              sure

                                    as the sun any

sane man can                                                    see no sin

            in the net of                          our life our

                        lies bodie s                    in situ in

                sand in                                        water geld

                                    the negro now

    and wash the                                  water of all sin

            èsù                                            oh l eau

                        l eau wash

        the water                        wash

                the water èsù oh                        èsù

                            save

                                    the                  us

            in you the ius

                                        in us

    no sin no                        sane man can no            sane men au

            sein de in

                                    the midst of gore

        de goré e sing

a song                                for rose un

        son la son le                            son for

                rosa a san                man                    for rose they

                hoe                        the field the toad

                            hops his ship                on

    the lip                                of ruin her

            every  where                            his hip his

        sore toe                too                much                    port rest

            rest rosa                            a hero rosa

        says                    is ever                    alone

                                the deed must

            be done rest says                        rosa me

    want fu                        fu omi

                                water the dread            deed dare

d                & done drat                            the cat dear

    ruth dear dear                        ruth i                        won her was

                wont to                        bed her bet

ten then                forty

                        guineas first an

ace

                of spades the deuce              it was that

      got me her forty             days nights forty          times forty

sins can              a man                  cede

            his soul

     no she             won t at night        the rings

in           her nose her            ear s shine

  the perils of          ripe lips a firm

      form bare          ass skin *il doge*

        the laird my liege      lord

            dives        amid

          the din the

dice the forty            *cedis* she bend s

      over the pain my

god my                   god why

            *olu seyi olu*

*seyi* hast        thou my son only

    a lad more                to me than tin

ore & gold *oh oh*     *omi omi*    *omi* oh me oh

    my god the cairn    *mei lua*

      mark s

the place we            met the ferns

    where i hid the         rings ruth our

      lips between cain

and abel a pact          of pain between

    her and me the          song *so la*

*fa so*         *la* far *isola*         *g long*

     *g long*         *g long*

  gong gong we ate     dates with rose     water the man

    in the red        fez and i        to

the east the            sun the dunes

      & gold

  tunis it is        a yarn i

    spin a tale       to be

      told not         heard nor

  read            a story that can

        not be        un

told we were

a good                                                    team sam

and me no              land no land no

more

land

for                                    the *san*

of the sand *me*

*wale me*                              *king son run*

*run save omo save*

*omo save omo omi*

*oh omi oh more*

*omi oh me*                              *beg* the vessel

rises it falls

the sea red

as wine rid                                    me of these

pests they              be

long to the              caste

of ants mis                                    taking gin

for water they mis              took

water for gin in *mi*              *tête*

*pot is mi ju*                              *ju mi obi* re

verse the age                    can we the

time the asp

appears the toad              hops the oracle

lives in the                              omen the lisp

of *ave s* vesper                              verses lap

lap lap lap

lap water cast                              the net

wide for lies                              to

found truth in the hand              s

pan of pain that

is s

pain a  round

the globe *mi orbe*

*de oro* bring                              the slop pail pin

her hold her

legs wide wet

her throw              water the shelves              a mess i

had an eye              a very good

eye           for                             negroes i grade

    them only      the best            a runt here

          or there the dog           star

     over us i                write i nod i

       write beg                 god drown

         my sin s in

rum reel about                 the deck a raw

    deal weal s on her            skin they lash

       her am spent

  now ruth can

     write no more salve       or raw skin *salve*

*salve* slave she

        reads & *ògún*           makes

          men

of iron ration              the beer &

    the amen s the veal          pies too

   & don t

       serve gin to the pig

the line           of negroes wend s

its way to     the coast i saw

  a star the      dog star i set

    my path by      it i  master

     captain & there       is long ing

   for

the north for        the aster & for

    the rose sip         sipsip wa

  ter wa        ter

    *omi* lap lap mis      fortunes

      rape this voyage     *mi*

*orí mi orí mi*        *head ma*

  *ma scene the same*

      *sea* ague gripe

     grips the       gut the gun

         get the

   gun the man   runs she runs

hold them over

    board with them    a rout it

  was a riot good       dog he     pats it *me*

    *i be*         *man me man*

                    *me san me*
*lua*                                          thugs all fins
        all round port                                  side star board
                fore & aft i am
        against                          sin shun crime                    i must re
                sume my tale fins                        all
                                                round the guinea
        negro pray s a name
                                                a name what
                        is his name he
        is *fon* he                              says i re
                main man though                          sin owns me the road
to rome is long                                  & my thirst
                for truth grow s *o*                      *rí orí or*
*i onise es*                      *o es es*                              *o es* you
        my must now                          my loss she
                has died coins                        on her eyes cradle
        the head linen for her                        bod y ease my
                mind ruth she was                        too thin hang
                                        him over
                        board throw her                    him too rum
        more rum time                        meet s truth in a pot
                of yam a
                        song an ode                        to the ne
                gro in me in                you to the one
                        the *son* the                        song in
                                negro i have                    lost ruth round
        and round sound                        of guns they run
                        dogs run to                        ground not
                        so not so
        tups her then                        tips her o
                ver in my gut                fear gut her them
                        too the raven                        nest s in *mes*
                        *rêves* rome
        mourns                                her ruins her
                runes some mourn
                        the dead we
                                the facts the

lives *i*

*lé i*　　　　*fè il*　*é ifè il*

　*é ifè* if　　　　　　only *ilé*

　　*ifè* we　　　　　　　　led

　　　　　　　　　　　　　　　them

　　　　to the　　　　rim o

　　　　f life a sure　　　ruse & ruin

of insurers such　　　　a loss such

　　　a sin we had　　　　　notes

　　　　of payment *wa*

　　*àgbò wa àgbò*

　　　　*wa*　　　　　　　*àgbò* my

　　　son my son i

seek the oracle　　　　of the

　　owl we had scone s　　　for tea once

　　　seen the queen

　dies stone　　　　scones hard

　　dry we rescue　　　　our tears

from the sea se　　cure them by writ o

*ra ora o*　　*ra* pray rail　　against time the

age against pope

　　　& nation against　　　*l*

*état* the　　　　state against flag

for *òsun*

　　　fowl *iya*　　　*iya* m

a ma *ema* we　　　eat what

　　is dead this

　　story turns

tail runs　　　from the truth each

　　word a stone

to turn o

　ver &　　over lose find

　& lose aga　　in to fall from

my lips &　　sink through

the deep to the ruin　　&

　　　rune

of bone there are

suits there are　　writs liens

& notes le *mot*

just *e* the just        word just

a word *ave*        *ave* to

the negroes and

*àse*        the wonder her

sex wet we sail

west with        the wind then east

up the wind

desire me make        me make her i

will *i*        *lé ifè*

a vision we supped

veal with wine        here

is a rope hang

him *ora* pray oh

poet of try

& troy of trope

& rope her feet

*un ange* we fearing        the sea her feet

ran fore ran        aft fins fore

& aft negroes

fore negroes aft tap

tap stag

and deer such a grand        garden an eden

a stage from there        to

sing to the        stars *à ma*

*santé à ta*        *santé à vo*

*tre santé*        come a stirring

air a song a        tune sapphire ear

rings for you my

once my upon        a time queen        a lace

ruff too eyes        stare the fuse

of this

story his story

is long cuff

them africa s sap        runs free sop

to insurers soap

the negroes oil        & feed them with a grout

head for a captain

& daft        too louts for a

crew we sail

to the indies only                       the owl s eyes can

                  see through the night

of this tale the noise oh                  the noise gold

           and sapphire for

you sue for me              a  pension bone

        of my bone song             of *le sang sang*

           of my *sang* the last

to die are the eyes              we eat lotus up

          and down up

     and down he        strode trod

   the board s as if               he owned

      the ship i am in

orders i can pray           for their souls pray

     for your own              master i pray this

       is my due from goré e

they came to             spill upon the seas a dare

    to the g

         od s *n*

*yame*                  *ò*

    *sun* we          d

      are you save                   us

        a rough band

of negroes             rush us mark

    them her make             me mark me

            too hot

      tongs irons she s done

for where           my *ju*

    *ju iye ny*          *ame* in an age

     of rot dire

          with peril &

      danger why             are they why

is she here          why are we

    in this tale this           story his story

      save her i can

not salve her          sores i author

     my own

      fate *nommo* is           my

   na               me

       & my n

ame is                                          *nommo* is water

                        is word was

            a den a lair                                          of liars on

                        the ship that set

        sail where from                          you ask africa

                i say how in                                  side the wind

clams feed on

                                    weeds weeds feed

        on bodie s we wend                          our way can

                    you not hear the noise                    ruth band of

        negroes run                          to and fro ship

            sail ship              sail how many

                    men on board                          ship sail

        ship sail how

                        many negroes over

            board her scent on                    my fingers my hand

                        the scent of

        africa is with                    me ever                on

            my skin my

                        lips your scent

        of rose s ruth                          in

                my mind only                          the rose s of war

    do not last grow              sere we feed

                them *àse* then                    feed the sea *àse*

        with them *àse*                          bodie s limbs

                    a frenzy of *àse*

            fins round                    and round *àse*          my gard

                en my eden                    fish sup

                        on the g

            ore in goré e who                          can save me

                        ruth how

                can sane men when

    truth is worn                          thin my word

            is my truth now                          drab

                        faded of no

    worth we must              we must i shed

                my skin as does                the asp am

                    no more who              i was or am *san* s


114

skin raw with                                    out the sin

              of s

                         kin in this age                    of gin rum

          & guns this age                         of *los negros les*

                         *nègres* ignore the age                      the rage of sane

men just                                     us ruth just

              us just *ius*                                        these are sad

     days over me                    *un ange noir*

                                   *niger* from the niger

              with wings do i                              exist is it

                         i i am ex

              man the sea                       is now a bod y

pond and she                   the one i                        desire who arouses

              me an agent              of satan of

                         lust is no                        more i exit

*la mer la*                                        *mer* every

              where *mare* these                              are sad days how

                                   many the ship

     appears a pig           sty sacks of corn

                                                       & grain des

              troyed water                   gone did we care

to spare them                    their fate us                              ours our fall

          they grow                          wings

                   *des ailes*                          *las alas*

                         we be                     do *ebo*

*for orí* we be                          use rum gin                      some corn she

              is mine no                         mine i had

     one queen                      the king                      a two

              of spades                     but she is my

                         queen                          my del

                              ta queen                          yo

                                   u spare *wale*

                    *sade* & *ade fon*                        *lua san ibo & e*

*we* we dis                              covered them

          all man                              negroes she

              negroes firm

lips put our mark s                      on them hot

              irons raw                              skin no cloud

                         sun over

head *scene enter*         *il doge his red*

     *robe parts* we         ate cured beef

& spuds         that night they hold

her who won         her if only i

had an ace wear         and tear of water

on bone a short         stint on a ship

a slave ship         was the lad s desire

just shy of seven         teen there were for

tunes to lure         a man from sane

to mad there         were perils pus

and bile      he died      the lad

ben of ague      told me he had      a

girl with gold      hair blue

eyes and a         smile do you

take this she         negro to be

y our s

lave y our queen

bell the cat         there are rat s

on board i do i         saw a sin so

large

as to make      you cry      & a man

of you there is now

a lien on my

soul

*à*

*se àse*         of words

& water carries         a ship yet drown s

a man is not red         yet turn s to

wine eats meat         on bones turn s

bone into sand         were we u

sed dupes      all to king      & state to pope

& *il doge*         to laird & lord

but abel is         dead there is

no bail for cain rise      rise sa

lute the lust      for africa the sound

of the lute stirs

the air & my lust         for gold for

guineas strum the lute      and

sift the dunes of

tunis for the bones                                    the ruins of my

                story their s & y ours

                                        our story it hides

        the secret that                                        in the rift between

                        cain & abel there

rome founds her                                self on murder &

                on death come                                        strum the lute some

                        more for my late

        soul *sum*                                *sum sum  sum* i am

                *sum* i am i        am *sum* sum

                                        of all ned

                s story no more

than eleven when                                he ran a

                        way to sea not                                that far from the lisp

                        of ma

ma pa                                pa he too had

                heard of  a seam

                                                of gold so

                        broad & so

        wide in an age                                of lust what

                        are we

        to do but lust

                                                let

                us wed then ruth

                when the ship sets                                me d

own on land                                again and

                        be done i                                am a new

                man sift the air                for enemies

                        of my soul                they are many sh h

                hush can you not

        hear the plea s                                        we were deaf to

                how to                                mend this i am

god s agent here                        on earth our rule                                is

                just and                                                we

                        must but                                to err so far

                from reason                it is a leaky tale i

                        recite it                        holds no water with

        map and wind                rose and a lamp

                to see them                                by we set

        sail crates                of portginwinebeercider                & water there were spuds live          fowl pigs

even how long        have we been       gone

too long we are       lost this is

a tale with the s

ting of truth in       its tail on her

finger i tied       a ring made

from string for her       my queen *afra*

*nigra* she       throws it over

board has on her       finger a red

string for *san*       *go* she says

and dives

once       queen

*regina* smiles

and dives ruth pray       for me ruth pray s

for me i

pine for her i       fear to tell this

tale on the river       delta the niger

i saw a sa

ble skin so rare       i long to pet it

they grin be

fore they dive       or fall grin

and die all

of eleven and

dead ned he

too had the       ague we have

thrown him over

board we pray then       throw him pray

then throw       them pray then

throw pray then

throw pray for       us or them

what no seer could

do the winds       did they stop

us have been gone

too long       the captain him

self is at sea       with the will

in sure the how

in rule we set

sail with reason       only to lead

us to seek the       lure in for

tune to find

only fear and who

we are flip

her over flop                    flop splash dive

dive my queen she

dove on a wing                let me di

ve too                                        let me

die the hen

ran the cat                ran the rat            ran the ne

groes ran the tongs

the irons marry me                            i beg

you there was                            no hate no

spite only                a job for a mad

king on his throne                rouse them all

strip and oil                them this my song                            of

rage to an age                            out side of time

where the sage live s

the seer who see s                            & does not

say it is                                                    the age

i tell you not                the man did

she falling find                            a rose find a

frica under

water a sad sound                the oud on

eid east                                is west &

west east where                sand meets the set                        in sun there

we sang sad                            songs sand

songs can you not

hear the sound                            of sand ruth

on bone we plant                            the stems of ne

groes in the seas                such a grand gard

en a red dawn                            covers us

we will

make the land groan                with grain and corn

dance with the sounds                            of grouse dove s

and tits *enter*

*il doge he takes*                            *off his red*

*cape puts on*                            *his sable one*

*the scene*                *begins* we

sail a boat                            down the niger

                    to the sea                                        port we have
    on board slaves                        on the beach
              at dawn i                                saw them the
                    negroes clad only                          in skin idle i
        stone the dog                              what did they
                owe us nothing                              round us the
                              earth groans                          sobs
        groans again                                with the weight
                    of rain i wait                                for the blue
          night under                        its cover i see
                    her the *ange*
              the sable one                                            with wings
    at first                              light she is
                    gone was it                          fun only a for
      tune to be had                        it had to
                be done at dawn                  of day the dead
                    lay dead *in*                              *situ* under
        water she tempt s
                              me spins
                a top falls ga
          ping apes all there                          was a gap
    in time be                        tween then &
                now where this tale                  exists *il doge*
                    has got
                              the gout too
        much port he nods                              he snores the tome
                    falls parse
              the crime not                        the sin parse
                    & praise
        the negro who gives                          us this day
                    our bread *le*
              *sang le* song                *el son* the deal was
          to begin                        & end in
                    time and we are out
                              of time lost like the
    ship it veers                                from one
            side to the
                    other i hear
              the sirens re                cite my verses they

lure me                                    on with my own

words to wrap                    me my only

help the *moly* you                    gave on the al

tar to my god a vase            of red rose s i fast

i pray hone                                    my *mea*

*culpa s* my *te*

*deum s* they rip her                    garment her paps

hang dry she                                    falls we graft

scions of africa in new            lands their sap

ours i hold fast

to my mind it  slips

falls in be                    tween *aleph* and *beta* i

lose it only                                    a gap

ing hole where it

use d to be o poet

of troy re                    cite your verses i take

my rum ne            at *à*

*se àse* the rain

ran red they fled            the fields

the negroes we            ran after                    them to the river

only a reed                    raft *san*

*go oh* hit  her                    over & o                    ver with her loud

sobs a mob bam            bam such

loss on a shelf

the mad king s calm

bust stares                    at me an urn *dan s*

*ma chambre sur*

*le lit* on the eve                    of the day i can't i

can my name i                    have

lost                    my name so much

to gain his wiles in

duced us                    me them the crew                    *o*

*rí orí* we sat                    on the moss Ruth

in the fen it was

wet on the eve                    of the day i left

you *me i name*                    *sade me wale*

*me*                    *omi tola me i name*

*ogun*

*ba my iya*                    *she be*

**121**

                    *queen* my name                              is
                              ted is dave is jon              is tim is
          alf is piet is peter
                                                       ishansistomisjim
                    issamisroyisdonisned                              is mike is
*esse* is *posse*                              is can ah but
              it s a rum
                              tale not for yo u
          ruth or yo u                                        clair or
                    yo u rose or yo u
          eve or yo u rosa                         or yo u                         clara
              yo u eva                              yo u tara or
          sue yo u              mary may mir yam
              or sara or yo u                         yo u or
                         yo u *scene il*                         *doge*
*dapper evil*                         *and rival to the king*
                    *appears exit*
          *the king* i dare                         you hold her
                    over board make
                              me never loud
          cries loud                                   snores at tea that day
                    he said we set
              sail to eden              and its end found
                    only eve *afra*
*nigra* no                                   deer read this a
                    sale of slaves thurs
          day oil them use                         beef fat or
                         lard *scene*                    *the snores of il*
*doge* sire  s                              pare me what
                    reason no sane man              should *de mans cam*
*tek me we want fish*                    *for inle & corn*
          *& sand* the raven
                                   comes she wants
                    my soul *mon*
          *âme* you have                              my *cœur* she has
                    my *cœur* the raven
soars i hear                              voices she has
                    my soul fear
          grips me my rictus                         smile i hear
                    voices *fa so*              *la fa*

122

*so la fa*　　　　　　　　　　*me so la* she

　　　　calms me don t

you see is　　　　　　　　　she dead has she

　　　　gone we seek

　　to tame them ta　　　　　　　　　　　　me her

　　　　　　for me & for you

　　　　tame her we

　　meet we mate　　　　　　no need to wed

　　　　no meat no

*pan* no *pain*　　　　　　no no it can

　　　　t be a sin overboard　　　　with you fish

　　feed bit　　　　　　by bit turn meat

to bone sea　　　　fans def

　　end the dead *orí o*

　　　*rí gbo mi*　　　　*mu* my queen she

was but a toy　　　　the story can　　　　not stand the

　　　　　　t

　ruth only *el*　　　　*son el son* my

　　song long　　　　　ago a tale was

told with no　　　　begin or end where

　　s the port and what

　　　　my part come　　　men the gin

the rum read

　　　　　this ruth and die hey

　　a pint of beer long ago

a tale was told

　　　　　　　an ass and a twit

　he was

Ferrum

*There was a noise and behold, a shaking . . . and the bones came together,*
*bone to his bone . . . the sinews and flesh came upon them . . . and the skin*
*covered them above . . . and the breath came into them . . .*
*and they lived, and stood upon their feet.*

EZEKIEL 37: 7, 8, 9, 10


*Praesens de praereritis.*
*The past is ever present.*

ST. AUGUSTINE

me i sing song

for *ògún el* *son* of iron come bring

our mask s

let the play begin we each act the part

in murder what will they

how do they the bones

say what cannot be give voice to

a tale one tale their tale

how bone be

come sand be

come the tale that can not be

told in this tale the *tao*

the way of the dead of what do

es this mean drat

that rat it ate the cat or is

it the cat that ate the rat halve

the ration of cod the globe

spins a top of

the possible help help i can t it

is late t oo lat e the oracle

where

lives the asp fore

told the for tunes and misfor

tunes how many lashes sire as

many as you

care to the bell peals the gong

sound s *oraora* *ora* pray i

beg you shave them all over their

head s their limbs their arms oil

them the asp crea

ture of secrets writ large slips from her

skin do not be sad dear ruth

you are my muse my must my

can in my mind s eye i see the

dales the glens the asp

leaves in the wind i spy i spy

with my aged eye something that

begins with m they

are tense sweat                    their fear weal s on

          teats on arms                              peat fires

                    in the bog be nice

     to me i beg she                    turns her

               head her                         lips from me i

                    slap her it s

          only an                    act a part

we play tears          sting my eyes i stub          my toe salute my

          king the nation          the flag use the salve

               to heal the skin can          we heal this

     sin with salve *tais*                    *toi* do

                    you hear a

          bove or                    is it un

               der the roar                    of

water their song *aide*          *moi aide*          *moi* help

          me help me i          can t it is

     late too late          the *oba* sobs

               his loss *omi so*

*o ore omi so o ore*                    water did a good

          job me *ode* me                    spear lion

                    and deer me

strong *ode* a tory          of great power bo

          red me such that          i must gr

                    it my teeth

as if he did no          t he owns

          ships though          on such a night

as this we dan          ce d under the st

     ars you and i ruth they          dance too on bo

               ard there is rot

                         in my toe & rot

     in the age the scene          is my own no one

               but i c

          an play it i wish          a w

and to tempt          time turn it from now          to then while

     it rains  we          feast o

          n flesh she rips and          tears

               his cape does the news

stun you i am                    cured for eve

          r of good ask why

     we sack their liv          es when last

i saw they we　　　　　　　　re all stan

ding on deck his　　　　　cape is to　　　　　rn it

must be sew　　　　　　n there is sc

ent of mus　　　　　　　　k of negroes

where　　　　　　　s the pin

t  pot of ale sin　　　　　　g for me an aria

of　　　　　　the asp oracle　　　　　　of hope lord

and serf master　　　and slave god

and man you　　　and i all　　　　　meet in the no

de that is this　　　hip dear clair i

gnore this tale i must　　　　recite all

the same they　　　　suffered *omi o*

*mio*　　　　　　　*mi* o my go

d *o*　　　　*mi* water if

*ifá* can if　　　　*ifá* can

if only *i*

*fá* can all　　　　　　that rema

ins are

words i do　　　not ow　　　　n they t

read water　　　　　then they sin

k un

der the we　　　　ight of *a*

*men s  ave s*　　　*& salve s* the flag

falls a nation　　　　　mourns my fate

waits greets me

in what i　　　　s to come a he

ro rose　　　　　up from a

mong the ne

groes *exit the me*　　　*n the king reads then*

*doze s he hold*

*s a gold o*　　　　*rb in his right*

*hand* a b

ad brew this of unde　　　rwriters & loss there was

marry in greed

and profit they braved　　　　the water get

the oar s there　　　was rush there

was roar there

was water arms　　　flail limbs　　*un bras u*

*n pied*　　　fail him up　　　there  a spear

in his side thur

sday is stud                                          day rut

        day the crew gets                                    up to antics

                              me i be

                  g you no                        throw *ayo* sh

    e big                              big *mi o*

              *mo* we can l                              ease slaves ask

                      the notary in t

        his time be                            yond help we

fall to                        our fate they

      to the o                          cean their fate

            & grace hold                              the candle up me

  n so i can              see i mad

        e a rush                    ring for you ruth

              *wale* make s a rush                    ring for *s*

    *ade* enter                    *the kin*                        g *he we*

        ar s red r                            *obe with a g*

            *old hasp* s                            o much s

    hit and b                        ile and p

            us the tare s  we                        re in the fiel

  d ruth *sad*                      *e* makes a ree                    d mat for *w*

        *ale wale* mak                        es a hut of ru

    sh                        and reed for *sa*                *de* the

                                                      stook s

    too & bog                                rush *wale* will we

        d *sade* the dray                            cart with ha

                  y where we t

  wo made o                            ne the cairn

            where i le                        ft a note

                  for you ruth *wa*

        le is *sade s* kin                        g *s*

  *ade* is *wale s*                  queen the o                men of *ifa*

        has no voice                  tar them kin

g at war with king              first tea with j                am buns *écl*

        *airs* bread an              d ham then

  i will as                k for your h                and am i

          n a j                        am j                        im sort t

        hem one fro                m the o

  ther hum hu                m shit pleas                to go

          d to rin                se the winds o

f per                ils make the sun san                e *de l eau de*                               *l eau* wa

ter *o*                     *mi* you say y

       ou capta                    in me i pa

y master o        ne cent for yo               u i he

    ar the cri           es a fist ag

       ainst he           ad a we

b of si           n traps m         e to sin

   with such e         ase *wale*

     and *sad*          e eat *fu*

*fu den de fun*        *fun dem c*        am ba

   *m ba*          m b         am d

    em ha         ve bi

g *gun* r        un *wa*        *le* ru

   n run *s*       *ade* ru      n see *wal*

    e run *sad*      e too at ves

per s i pr        ay no har        p or or

  gan *pa*           ter *pat*

*er j ai fa*      *im* will no o        ne hear me

   his so         n a spe

ar in his si      de thorns on his he

   ad red stain       on his s

    kin can he      turn s

our water bil     ge water into s    weet water g

   eld him c      ut cut all re

d now her e     yes two lamps    in my very

  own nig       ht we p

   lay at dice      for the be

    gin in new tim    e grows old

so do        es cir

  ce the crone t     he hag the

   seer a cast in her e    ye do

le out the bil     ge wat

  er they do      le the water do

le out the a    le they do    le out the al

  e we si      p port she la

 y in     ert we     als on the sk

   in no gar     ment to co

ver her o    r my si    n we sha    red her t

  he king mak    es a dec     la

   ration of w     ar so too the p

ope *il doge*                          the laird t

he lord again                                    st *wa*

          *le* and *sade*                              there are o

     mens in mis                          for

          tunes we sho                    uld no

te *wale* a                          nd *sade* w                    ill ha

     ve a                              son *a*

*de* is his na          me the kin                    g the p

          ope *il doge* t                    he laird and t

     he lord mak                         e a de

          clara                          tion of w

ar again                    st him too *orí*                *onise ada*

     *aye orí ape*                          *re* if only o

     mens lie                    d you and i ruth w

          ill have a so                    n dan

          te will b                         e his nam

e slam her                              head again

          st the bo                              ard s will

     no one he          ar me b                    ut dante po

          et of the li          fe after death h          ear me o

h g                    od ro                    ugh winds

     rip the we                    ft of *wa*

*le sad*                              e & *ade* th

     ere are we                          als on *wale s* s

               kin *sade s*

          & *ade s* too                    enter the kin

g red ro                    be gold th                    orns on his he

     *ad a man ge*                    lid as the north                he

          *comes from* if                    we cede the is

les to the kin                          g of spa

     in what have we w                    here can *wa*

          *le* and *sade* hid                    e in time in

the p                              ast can ca

     in can cai                              n can & did d

                         o a

     bel cain c                    an cain ca

n & ab                    el is not a y                    arn a t

     ale a sto                    ry that can

          t can co                    me eat sip

     and su                    p at this tal

e that can t c          an a sa

d tale it          is i ran          t i ran

t run fro          m the sun          s rays i am h

am h          am i a

m i a          m cur          se o

f go          d by g          od cur

se d as          they are h          is so

ns of nig          ht thr

ow          n out          side of ti

me ha          m i am          that

i a

m do          not be c          oy with me

ruth i b          eg you *let*

*us have a ne*          *w act a new s*

*cene new a*          *ct new sce*

*ne* so here          is dido she

discove          red the save

in africa          find s a hid

e found s a          city again

st ro

me and the vise

of time *w*          *ale* and *s*

*ade* g          row          g

rain to ma          ke beer *the kin*

*g sits on his da*          *is on his is*

*land read s a pa*

*per tha*          *t says he o*

*wn s negro*          *es man*

*y man*          *y man*          *y negroes* we din          e on

egg drop so          up eat fish

roe fe          ast on dat          es from

the e          ast cure

d ham & beef the ne          gro serves fresh p

ears on a tray

with my pro          fits ruth

we can ma          ke gin

with the g          rain in our fie

lds circe and her sire          ns sin

g their son          gs tempt wit          h all t

here is          to eat the *san*          can sin

g they dance                    too haw                    ham i

s where i              live a sad s              ad land this i

s land where ti              me sag s wh              ere i sail fro

m to serve m              y kin

g you al              so serve rut

h who sit s              and wa

its on time how l              ife fli

es we we              re ma

king gain              from the        m to sin

k all we had in s

kin le

g irons              on hi

m her too i want              you to li

ve in e              ase ruth cl              air cla

ra ro              sa etc where

meet *a*              *leph* and the o

m in o m              y god my

god a he              ro  a

rose a sh              e rose we              must cure the

m of a              frica w

here be

gins the lon              g in g              one where o

ld and n              ew are but

words our fort              unes are              at s

take the ship              glide s m              ist all

round *les nègres*              *sont gens pas*

thin

gs *pas co*              *sa s pas pas*

*the loan of his*

*pani*              *ola to the king*

*has gone*

*bad* me *o oni*

me be kin              g me i

as              k you sp

are *iya omo*              me i              pa

y gui              nea for *omo*              me i sa

ve the              m *je rêve j*              *e rêve i*

*l rêve* do              you *rêve* ru              th

beg

in where it              be

gins there i        s no such        where he

i only        tell a sto

ry it c        an not be tol

d *dem gi*        *ve tiki tiki fo*

*ini fo tai*        *tu fo ma*        *i*

t        he king en        ters gold on his he

ad the cre        st on his se

al is g        *old* the see

r peer s into ti        me to come sees no

thing sees only        time to come *isola*

*i so la mi*        *so la mi fa*

*so la so*        *la* this i

s how the so        ng go        es where the

bee suc        ks there        do the s

ums ma        n fifty ne

groes        take away ten        leaves how man

y *cedis* her        in my l        ap a g

irl betwe        en lisp and s        lip the slip

of  his ro        be red we s        lip them st

em from roo        t pare them d

own for a gar

den never see        n where be

gins the eve        r in ti

me the bell sounds        gon go

ndo n do  n they        give us s

lip are go        ne be

fore we ca        n say o

ver wit        h you the s        um of six

ty & for        ty is ze        ro cir

ce the cro        ne s

it s a        top a pi

le of bones

me *o oni* m        e king yo        u kin

g  we be        ki

ng you sp        are *omo mi so*        *la iso*        *la*

*mi*        *isola m*        *on ile je rê*

*vejerêvejerêvede*        r

uth *the k*        *in*        *g wa*

nts to        *ma*        *ke*

*lo*        *an of*        *his pan*

i          ola h                              e holds

t      he has              p o                              f his ca

pe                    h                    is g                              old o

rb                    h                    er in m

y lap sk              im the s

kin of the se              a *la*                    mer ma mer

el *mar ma*              *mère mare*                              for e

yes l                    egs ea              rs h

ands hea                    ds & f              eet f

or bo              die s l                    im

bs for ri                    bs spin                    e s to

es shi        n s & lip                    s for pel

vis              & fe                    mur

for                    mo      lars f

or *ho*              *la* &

hey *ave* &

sa                    *l*            ve for i

c              a              n                    i can for i

am *je*            *suis* & *yo*                    *so*

*y*

for *sum*                    e              go & *eu*

*sou* scan                    the se              a the w

inds for the ta

te te ta ta for tum                    de tum for

a be

at *o*                    *bi obì mi*

*o*

*bì ifìn* sa              ve me na              ils in his p

alms nails              in he                    rs red *fa*

*so*

*la mi*

so la re          *mi so la fa mi*              *from i*

le *ifè* m              *i from o*            *ya olú*

*fe*              *mi o*                    *lú*

*seyi* skin              kin

g &              queen of kin                    we

t her tie                    her by the h

eel her nails                    ra

ke my s                    kin she s

pit s s how did w                    e get in

to this me                                    ss *act s*

                    *cene anger*

        *mark s the kin*

                              g s *mien his an*

            *ger is dan*              ge                    *rous we must*

*have ca*          *re* they lie                  on shel

        ves logs              tied one                      to the other oh

                the sin of i                  t all hush can

        not let t              hem hear me ru

            th spin

    the globe turn                      it un

                der your h              and see how f

            ar we have          go                      ne scan

                the wa          ter for *el*            *pa*

        *n de vi*              *ta* bread          of li

            fe fo                      r bo          nes to      e bon

e he                  el b                  one l              eg bo

    ne hi              p bo                  ne ha              nd b

one a              rm bon

    e no                      se bo                  ne e

            ar b                  one fin              g

        er bon                                e hea

                d bo                              ne bon

    e bone all          is bo                  ne wha                      t be t

                        he be

            at in b                      one how

                say the o

    racle bones *eyo*                  *ba eyo ba*                  *ah eah*

            *lo ong o*                      *ba ka*

            *ka serah*                          *foh*

                *la ahpa serah foh*

    *egon egon sura*                          *sha* there

            is be                              at in bone

                the                  re is go

    ne in bo                  ne you wish                  to wed e

        sau a dower gi                  ft for you gr

                ace a fine she                  negro now i no

    d my eye                      s drown dow

            n down dr                              own the won

der the *wun*              *der* of under wa

ter what ra                                              ce of me

          n this ni                 g nogs                              of guin

ea how man                      y guineas                  for this gui

          nea man once the              re was on                    ce up

on a ti                              me *il*                    *y a hay*

                              *& est* ro

me tro                                                          y & si

                    on there was

                    on                                              ce now she

re                    ad s rapt th                      is story

        yarn a tale                    which w

              ill not be                      told yet w              ill have it

s say it                      is a wh                    ore age w

        here all li                    ve by evil how              ca

              n we ye                    t we do we

grip                    e we gr                              in we grie

    ve the                          n gr              in a

          gain fez                  lives aga

    in in              the m                    in

                    d and the *o*

          *oni* of *oni*                              *se* rides int

                    o war for                                          neg

        roes for sla                            ves how man

y *rotls* f                            or this guine                  a man he

        asks we eat pi

                              g pies por                  k with sage

              and sion so                  me port she

reads no                  mo                    re of the a

        ge of ho                    w wh

              y & whe

        refore of who              res who                  serve

                                                              tim

    e & pee              r into t                  he past          at ves

          pers tho                  ugh they sin

g of nigs              and of  no                          gs and s

        in hey herb              cast of                    f the gri

          pe s hans cut                  the rope s scion s

of ro                              se and ye

    w of af                          rica we had

          with us s                            lip s to gar

den with the tin

es of ti　　　me grip th　　　e past w

ill not let　　　it go　　　or me

be nor will

i o　　　ver the se　　　a amen s of ves

pers rin　　　g out & o

ver cries  o

ver sho　　　uld o

ver could　　　and no o

ver & ov　　　er & o　　　ver miss cir

ce takes a sci　　　on of the herb si　　　on

with so

me sage *pate*　　　*r* i wi

ll lift mi　　　ne eyes *sin*　　　*me sin m*

*e sin me* with　　　out me sin

g the vesper ver　　　ses ring the

m out loud o

ver the wat

er *il doge sci*　　　*on*

o

*f rome sin*　　　*gs at ve*　　　*spe*

*rs of n*　　　*igs and n*　　　*ogs* there

was

ague the　　　re wa

s grip

e there w　　　as fren　　　zy th

ere was e　　　vil there　　　was a

men a　　　nd *a*　　　*ve* there was *me*

*a & cul*　　　*pa* t　　　he

re was gr　　　ieve  & wo　　　e

si　　　n th　　　ere w　　　as

no

is　　　e of neg　　　roes oh th

e no　　　is　　　e there wa

s pro　　　fit the　　　re was

loss  there　　　was ga

in t　　　heir loss

*ayo*

*do ague*　　　*fo mi* who　　　wh

o ho　　　o h　　　oo o　　　men o

f                     owl & a                    sp *ye*

*ya ye*

          *ya ye ya*                    *ah y*          *e ye ye*

*ye ah ye*          *ye* i ro                    de the ma

     re to me               et you th                    at da

          y on the da          le fi                    sh sup a

     fin               ger her               e a le

     g there ma               ke the               ir ho

          me in bone o          racle bones ah          wo o

ah wa ah                    wo wh                    ere is *wa*

     *le sa*                    *de* too a

     nd *a*                         *de* whe

re the hu               t of ru                    sh ree

     d and red               mud w

          here the ree               d mat *sade* ma

ke s for *wa*               *le* who car               es for *a*

     *de*  now &               then *a ah who*

          *o ai ye ee* wh               at is the ti

     me where be               the be

          at in bone sir               en s call t

          empt with son               g all night

     a stir                    ring son

          g  to mak          e my lo                    ins sti

          ff har          d with de          sire to fi

re my lust          the sir                    en s song

     *fa s*               o la l          a la m

*i fa*          *so r*          e re d          *o do mi*

*f*          *a so so la*          *do* on bo

          ard we ha          d spu          ds win          e por

t ru               m ha          m corn & rice          i have to

     ld you a               ll that be               fore & wa

          ter

to se                         cure our pro

     fit we th          row them to res          cue our for

          tunes we          do mur t               hey f

     all to in          sure our pr          ofits ov

          er & o          ver a                    gain to sec

          ure their re          scue the               y fall o

ver bo               ard to pre          serve our profit

     what i               s bo               ne bu

t bone stone                    of then evi              dence of a pa

st drow              ned in no                      w p

lay on my bo                nes the son

g of bo              ne in b                      one sh h ca

n you he              ar  the be                      at in bone *pie*

                              *je*

*su pi*              *e jes*                  u sanctus santuc              sanctus ag

*nu s dei* in              san                      *ctus* there i

s *san* say              a *sa*                      *nctus* for m

e a *san*

*ctus* to the s                      ea a *s*

anctus to the *s*                      an san              s *san s*

san s s                      anctus i

am we a                      re their e

yes stare                      see thin              gs we ne

ver wil              l let my s                      tory my tal

e my g                      est gift ri

se up in ti                      me to sn

ap the sp                ine of tim                      e *pat*

er pa                      *ter* say a *pie je*

*su* for me                add a s                      anctus th

row in an *ag*              nu s dei p

ater for me a *mi*

sa una m                      isa how man

y gu                      ineas for a *mis*

a pate

r prat                      e the *a*

*ve ma*                      ri *a* pra

y *pa*                      ter pray f                      or me

for th                      em sa              y a *san*

ctus f                      or the s              ea but dr

own the can              t *pater* i                      t is do              ne lots

of *pi*                      etas to              o *pa*

ter

                              &*fi*

des & sp                      es dum d

um de du                      m dum  th                      e no

ise the                      noi              se th

e drum it do                      es not sto

p the o                      ba so                      bs a

141

gain what d           eed this

hat cree           d have we cre

ated in our nati      on of cards      we sa

il the se      as to the e

ast sat      in the we      st the in

dies go      ld and t      in she s

erve s us a d      ish of s      puds wit

h so      me sage

& a sci      on of the her      b sion o

ut of the d      eep *p*      *ie jesu*

*pi*      *e je*

*su* our cr      eed of no no

t & new b      less me *pat*

*er* i a      m sin *o*

*rí o*      *rí or*      *í o*      *ni*

*se* they      hug the      y fa

ll *la m*      *er ma mer m*      *a mèr*

*e* wh      ere does di      do fl

ee to a      frica what do      es she ther

e she fo      unds a cit

y why do      es did      o flee she see

ks a pla      ce to rest      an a

cre of ho      pe in a hide

where is d      ido g

one to g      round in afri

ca *wa*      *le* and *sade* u

sed to li

ve in af      rica did

o flees to afric      a seeks a

place to re

st an a      cre of hop

e in a hi      de to f      ound and g

round a c      ity hip h      op hi

p ho      p the to

ad ho      ps its pa

te bare a r      uby in its l      ips it i

s a story i      cy c

old in i      ts de      ep s th

eir eyes star      e at u      s how m

any s      uns are there i      see si

x me i h          ave ten s

ons me big                    man me          asure the r

um & the lo                    ss in                    *o*

s in u

s in *i*                    *us* the s          hip veers to t

he west e          ver what d

o the bones          say ru

th the r          eed the ree          d us

e the reed          for a

ir *ma*          *re m*

*are* all i          s *mare* a

ll is se

a the          y quit ho

ld of the ro          pe fa

ll & s          o qu          it this li

fe par          e the spu

ds a          nd sp

are the ser          mon s tie

the fee          t se          w the ey          es sh

ut it i          s do          ne cap

tain d

rap          e the tor

so the li          mbs wi          th li

nen in my e

den the          re is do          ve t          it and rave

n ow          l too th          e ease

of i          t all t

he crew i          s no          t sa

d nor the c          apta          in a to

ad by ano          ther name i          s *un an*

*ge* a rub          y in he

r lips the su          n s dis

c hang s r          ed & ho          t ove

r us th          e sa          me ru

se the sa          me m

use you h          ow it gr

ow s the f          ear we hu

nt eat har          e in my ede

n we hun          t them t          hey eat th

ey shit i pla          ce my wi

g on my he          ad they e          at they s

hit my lo          rd my li          ege lord i sa

lute you w          e sit o          n the ru

g a go          od rug fr          om the e

ast from t          unis eat dat          es fresh f

igs mak          e musi          c with ou

d and tars ma          ke de          als for ne

groes with the m          an in the re

d fez fr          om over th

e gold dun

es rut

h my m          use i lo          ng for y

ou to hu          g me to          w row r

o          w row r          ow r

ow to          ad and t          it mo

use in m          y e          den *o*

*rí o*          *rí me b*

*e thir*          *st* reams of no          tes for y

ou to so

rt tend the m          are the toa          d hops o

f f into the n          ight drops its r

uby pen the p          ig pen the n

ig sing a          n o

de to ni          ght & to the s

in un          der the s          kin to s

ion nig          ht s vo

ice i          s wit

hout so          und the s          un ve

ers we a          re out s          ide of time and o

ut of ti          me dar

e to step f          rom trut

h to wad          e in de          ath in d

ying and di          do flees her fat

e to a          fri

ca finds i          t their fa          te o

urs ru          n to grou

nd their f

all our f

all i          t was a b

ull marke          t for g

uineas & gui                                    nea negro

es a b                                    ear mark

          et in h

   ope nig               ht fad                      es to da

      y da                          y to n

        ight her d            ugs ha          ng sa

cks of d             ry fe            ar ho          pe fad

   es to fe                 ar th            ey eat t

        heir fea                 r and all          roun

      d is f                 ear i mo

urn you mo          urn we mou          rn our *mo*

      *rt* they hur          t we w

ill have a big d          ish of s          puds with b          eef *el s*

      *on* the s                 ong we e                at we d

        oze she but a b          it a s                lip of a g

   irl we c                 ome to p          raise the r

      use in d                 upe they pr          aise *o*

*rí i*          *lé i*                          *fé* in a          n age so

   rare that p          hrase again the                 *oba* so

        bs with pra          ise and p                 us the sh

ip sail s o             n board s             aint sow & ca

      ptain p                 ig s                aint s

        in & lor                 d tin the v                essel y

   aw s first e          ast then we                 st i p

      ray to the e          ast the                n to the w

est to the n             orth & so          uth no e                vide

      nce of g          od but o          ur negro

        es have ya                          w s the y

      aw s le                 ak p                us

there is n                          o new t

        hing here on e                arth *de fun*

      *fun m*                 *an come t*

*ek we a*          *way* we li                 ve by old cr

   eed s ma             de new the                 more to su

        it our de                 ed s have the r

am tup the e             we i tup & t             op the q

      ueen of s                 pade s in our ede          n the pi

        g grouts r                          outs in the d

   ung  we sa                 il we

        st for e                 ast & e

den the capta       in a man o

f girth of har     sh  mien and vo     ice eve

n with the s     he ne

groes i s     aw him r     ub his s

ex aga     inst her i se     ek no g

old no     r tin no sap

tin sap     phire no     r rub

y nor the o     re of the i     ndies m

y eden is y     ou r

uth only y     ou *me i b*     e od

*e mo*     *i je suis*     *ode* we ca

me d     own the r

iver the     re was a f     ort in the mi

st wh     ere we wo

uld prove our mu     st our mig

ht & rig     ht there wa     s dew o

n the     ir ski

n on he     r sk

in he wa     s a sly o

ne with our guine     as we turn t

o the or     acle it tun

es our fort     unes wh

ere must cre     ates will th     ere ò

*gún* live     s a twi     t and a l

out to boo     t he pas

sed out o     n deck a

pes all th     ey shed t

ears fresh t     ears will not e

at sal     t will never s

ee a     frica aga

in they s     ay a s     cene neve

r seen b     efore & w

e are late in t     ime for the e

ast ede     n & eve

r *wal*     e and *s*     *ade* have no     hut i ca

n not b     ear this t     ale told b

are of all t     ruth ru     th you a

re my m     ust m     y can t

his story i     s not mi

ine to t     ell tell i     t i m

ust it was on        ly trade after a

ll *act s*        *ix sce*        *ne o*

*ne* we mat        e them a b

ill of s        ale for a b

ale of h        ay a gu        inea m

an a ne        gro *my fri*

*end i p*        *en this to y*

*ou since y*        *ou are my f*        *riend an*

*d will no*        *t* we fish for c

arp in the ri        ver ferns all r

ound *i w*        *ill eve*        *r brood on e*

*vents seen b*        *y me* to give m

y all to t        he nation b

ut i was cu        red of my l

ust for the s        he ne

gro they han        g on

with tw        o hand        s we t

ug they f        all f

orm un f        orms hal        f man hal

f ape h        alf man a        ll a

pe *i*        *fá if*        *á if*

*á* if o        nly *i*        *f*

*á*

after the r        am t

ups the e        we tie i        t to t

he mast o        n d        eck *àgb*

*ò* for *ò*        *sun* the bo        ard s ran r

ed from the r        am *le s*        *ang* for *òs*

*un* sin        g sin        g si

ng th        ey sing *fa f*        *a fa* i

f only *if*        *á* they li        ft the bo

die s ma        ke an a        ltar to *ò*

*sun* to s        *ango* we s        ing our *a*

*ve s* & *s*        *alve s* t

hat phr        ase a        gain the *o*

*ba* sobs *s*        *ame act di*

*fferent s*        *cene* they dr        owned *il d*

*oge* p        reens his to        e so

re with g        out the mo

ss on the s        tone where we s

it you a                              nd i rut

h and eat a d          ish of whe                         y we s

ail lead in t              he sail from a                    frica s c

oast to ow                        n now never eve

r & w                          ill we sa                        il for a far is

land for sunsh              ine se              a do

gs in a wo              rld of wa              ter the wo

nder of i              t all in h

ope that we le              ave sin              the sta

in              of ni

g and no              g is with u              s ever *d*

*iff*              *erent act sa*              *me sce*

*ne* they dro              wned the *ob*              *a* sobs a

gain & a              gain  that ph

rase god ch              arge s us w              ith their we

ll be              ing will he c

harge us with a c              rime *i*

*lé ife* li              ves no quest              ion s at s

unrise or at the f              all of the s

un the sun veer              s then q

uits *u*

*se her as y*              *ou w*              *ill she is n*

*ow y*              *our s*  *sin* s

in i a              m wit

hout sin b              ut we me              et be

come friend              s sea fa

ns dance se              a cre

atu              res ride the b

ones we rest              they re              sist the r

am is dead              *no res*              *cue to*

*day seas e*              *alm* sam calms

her wipes her              tears the

se creat              ures a se

cret race a qu

est so di              re i fe

ar the e              nd t

roy but a r              uin a ru

ne a secret s              ure and se

cure on th              is day i quest              ion the rise

in sun long              for night the candle

in its sc    once shows me    the way to her *que*

*es esto* what    is this wha

t do    es this me

an my ha

nd writ    es the rea    son his h

and writ    es the reas

on a pin    t of be

er some por    t to rin

se my s    oul of s

in can a b    at swim a s    in die the

y had mort    ality by the t

ail in did    o afric

a grafts r

ome to her a s    ecret so se

cret the b

ill was d    ue the no

te wa    s due sh    e was du

e o    verbo    ard wa

s no mo    re *la*

*d on the q*    *uay wan*    *ts to se*    *t sail for t*

*he ever in e*    *den does not s*    *ee all tha*

*t waits for h*    *im* fe    aring f    ear they

and we g    round on the re

ef of o    ur st

ory ear    rings o

f sapp    hire fo    r my g

irl rub    y too fea

ring her e    yes i run    her fe

et co    me af

ter me mi    ne enemi

es set upo

n me *il*    *é if*

*é* an e    gg for *ò*    *sun* it i

s hot in her    e piles & he    aps of fin

ger ring s n    ose rin

g s ear r    ing s the cre

w shares we din    e on me

at sip win    e *à ta san*

*té* dear r

uth *ma chè*

*re* ruth a fe                      ast we had *mis*

*e en scè*              *ne*   a shi

          p or v                    esse

     l the s                              ea man

          y negroes a ran

t of rains the                y ring they sin

     g they b                              eat u

          pon the d              eck ho

  ld the e                ar ring fast bo              y *so*

  *me neg*                          *roes had pil*

          *es leahy pile*                    *ı* the saint of tro

     y and the de          ad city ro

       me app                    ears to me

at night *l ang*          *e de me*              *r noir nig*

     *er afer* her s              ex we

  t her p                aps leak p      rop them u

     p *ilé*                    *ifè i*              *lé if*

*è il*          *é ifè* se              w the lin

     en slip sh          ut we ro              t in this ves

          sel from s              in sin

  g by rot          e a stir              ring son

     g their dy              ing grist & g              ift to u

       s *tō se*                *cure a pro*

*fit we u*                *se man*              *y ruse s*t

     heir swe              at the sce

          nt we stu              n the su

n with o              ur act it

     veers off i                ts way we

       let win              ter s frost  fr

  om her urn no *a*          *ve s* or *sal*

     *ve s* only sla                ves *às*

          *e àse* so b

       e it the so              und of the o

  ud on e              id fa

          lls on u              s on tu

nis a st          ring of n          egroes on t

  he qu              ay no sou              nd the m

     an from f              ez wa

       its to se              ll to ma

  ke a de                al *the stì*

*ng of t*

*ruth is e*

*ver with m*      *e i ma*      *he y*

*ou a g*      *ift de*

*ar ru*      *th of th*      *is she ne*

*gro her na*      *me is sa*      *de i cal l*

*her di*      *do u*      *se her as y*

*ou w*      *ill re*

ad the poe      t of t      rope t

roy & r      o

me *wa*      *le* and *s*

*ade* ma

ke      grist to b      rew b

eer whe      re r

iver me      ets se

a meets p      ort there stand

s a f      ort of n      egro

es the men w      ear no p

ants the sh

e negro      es have bar

e t      eats a m      ist co

ver s the fo      rt on the riv

er on the po      rt a l

ace ru      ff for my neg

ro and sat      in pants t

oo i mak      e you a g

ift of hi      m they p

ant they fa      int to plan

t a fla      g for na      tion & for k

ing to p      lant our s      eed my to

y for      t sits on a r      iver on a po

rt i p      lay at gun

s no s      lave s fire      no shot s

in nest s with

in come sir      my lie

ge lord it i

s now y      our turn co

me b      e me rains fa

ll no wa      ter in the tub    p

lay your p

art the sun rose

under sk

in sin for          ty days fo

rty nigh          ts forty *ce*          *dis* for forty

sins *j ai*          *faim j ai*

*faim* god of          spire *spes* and p

raise turn and          turn the bo          nes sing

a son          g of wa

ter a wat          er so

ng sin          g song sin          g song de

fend the d          ead & sin n

o sin sin          g the bo          nes h o

me what w          ill my b          ones say h

ow do the          y forty we

eks come to t          erm sh h *au*          *di* can you

not he          ar from the de

ep s the voi

ces not sir          ens we are a

t sea the d          art of my sto

ry stings i me

ant no harm          no hurt res

cue us rag          and bone men in

dict the a          ge pears in g

in in          wine win          ter wine and y

ou ruth          this story ne

sts in the ne          t the we          b of ti

me tam          p it down do

use the flam          e of this ta

le what pro          fit me if *mon*          *coeur non est*

we wind o          ur way sub          wa

ter thro          ugh bon          e bed s o

nly the bone          s of the sh

ip their e          yes dart this

way and th          at soft so

ft they ro

am the ship          their cri

es grate on m

y ears  drag          the dee

p s for the b          ones of my so

ul their sou          ls cast the n

et wide to the d          eep men to the dee

p and a                                tot of ru

          m for y                                      ou scu

                    m upon a ti                                        me at the be

     gin in nil                              e the bl

          ue nile a lin                          e of ne

                         groes gain t                        he shore w

   ill the sea                          give up its de

               ad its bo                              nes cob s of co

                    rn sacks of g

          rain by gra                    ce and by lar

                    d *père* grant u                          s this da

                         y our n

ig nig no                              g and so

          up a rash of s                          in it was hang

                    him overb

          oard throw h                          er never se

               en again mar                          ry time to t

                    ruth you t

     o me ruth the d                          un horse wa

               its under the t

          ree for u                              s cede the l

and grant us w                    rits *il doge* be

          deuced they p                    ray into wat

                    er what was d

               ue them but                    life i

   t self they wr                    ite on water                their c

          rie s their gro                    ans their sob

                    s their oh s th                          eir ahs ya

weh what was s

                         he worth *esta be*

               *lo lindo* my *geld*                          *is op* my mon

     ey spent she                    is y ou

               rs they ar                    gue water fle

     d water al                    ms and arms fo

          r the poet of t                          roy of the past

that is no and                    now who writes o

               n water this po

          em of lo                    ss the shape of th

               is now b                              ones to sand t

o clam s the tr                    ope that is tro

y is *de tro*       *p* my limb s a

che so to       o my he

ad i wish yo       u were he

re to sap i       t with rum t

o ease my m

ind the crew c       all them *bens*

*cosa s coi*       *sa s* thing s t

hey live with the e

el s now *op*       *en neer* piet writ

es to his ans

up and do       wn *op en ne*

*er* they ru       n *ik houd van*       *u* ever at the e

nd of tim       e go

ld tun       is they call on *d*

*anh* the rain se       rpent of ti

me they call *ai*

*do hwe*

*do* we d       raw straw s w

ant fo       r died n

egroes b

are arsed the

y f

all the d

hows set sa       il from tin

gis with stu       ff and sla

ves each g

rain in s       and each dro       p in water *or*

*i* oh he       al the sk       in of sin

the sin of s       kin sing

e the feet o       nly water with sc

um the s

hip lies id       le its bones gro

an to b       e with y       ou i

dle in our e       den sh h hear *de*

*bel* a sp       ear in his si

de *mi o*       *bi mi ob*

*i* it is but a ru       in of a sto

ry a rune       to found the f

ind in r       ome to fin

d the fou       nd in qu       est in

their d

ebt ever use          her as you

will they c          all his n

ame fall into t          he blue nig

ht they bra          ve the wa

ter sing a p

raise son          g that is a

frica un

der water a d          aft boy sim

ple in the he          ad he was o

ne grain of s          alt under *t*

*ong* in my mi          nd gr

ants of l          and to gr

ow cane & g          row ri          ch ruth

can you no          t hear the s

ound of s          and on san          d on b

one water be          ar s the t

ruth i run fro

m a run          e a ru          in of a stor

y to turn o          ver lose find in a          gain she w

ear s but her s          kin what a f

eat this t

ear fate grow s f          at with fe

ar this st          ory can not b

e my only s          on a lad po

our water o          n this s

in aga          inst time

we se          rve them ru

in wring the s          tory dry in

sure feet fus          tic bead          s tendo

ns & ham          string s can          dleslipsearese

yes even go          d and *les an*          *ges* spit *orí o*

*ri oh wa*          *le* come s h o

me *òrìsà* de

af to their cri

es can we m          end this ma

n this we g          ive them *le m*

*ort* the sea li

fe water li          ves they as

k for wat          er bread & l

155

ife for *ilé*                    *ifè* a fa

ir trade i

t was li                         ce mice f

arts and sh                              it her fe

et flit her

e and the                                re we use wil

es & spit                  e rose hi

p tea at the man              se sco

nes with j

am m                                    ind y our ste

p may their s

ouls rise from t                    he har

d water                              they be

ing the ro              ot sand ru

b s bone c                          lean so mu

ch heat

sun s be                    ams a story mu

st bear its we                          ight a la

ss of ten s                  he was t

oo thin b                  y far we bree

d then b                          ed them i

f they bo                  lt tie t

hem *ayud*                  *ame aide*

*moi* crad

le it to no                  ava                  il parse the n

egro pe                  st gna              t open and s

ift the ti              me sow the ta              res of s

in tears of ne          groes grow g              ibes all rou

nd eat gr              ub s the ca                  ul a ch

arm an a

rk of sou              ls under w                  ater we give or

ders they sta          re *fer*

*rum* th                  row *de bon*

*es dem* my          hope a spi              re to th

e sky we gi          ve the bon                  es order what

is she but          my story it d                  ies in tim

e & within          this tale time d          ies *from tun*

*is stuff so*

*fine y our eyes w*                          *ill shine my d*

*ear* i have *m*                  *es ordres* he

trod the grou                          nd of tro

y a king in rom              e too he stro

de we hunt fo              wl at the for

t eat sip beer              from gourd s farts

and other sounds              from mouth

and ass boast s

of gold and guineas ten              guinea negroes for

one sapphire for              you rose *j ai*

*faim* for ruth for t              ruth

*ius* is just

us              the yams were

bad they sail

on a red tide o              n a die

t of bad y              am and s

our water so              me fish co

me be me              for one day *lève*

*lève* rise te              *k mi ju*

*ju hold it sa*              *fe for i* i

t is *ius*              & just *how i m*

*iss the ci*

*ty* the s              he negro ent

ices me wit

h her scent traps              my lust my ho              pe for you

can a b              at how about a ra

t the scen

t of you ru              th wafts acros

s oceans *dans ma c*              *hambre le code*

*noir* my lad

y *noire* how i pet h              er *ifá* i

*fa ifá* the r              am tie i

t to the ma          st *le san*              g *le sang*

they sang i          sang of grace he              longs for gra

ce were w          e *ewe lu*          *a* or *fon* could

we come be m          e this my bo              d y my *sa*

*ng* my bon          e a rose bu              sh in the gar

den a sun r          ose in my ede

n *iye* i              ye *iye* the rose is now

sere *dis my ju*          *ju* you no

tek me *o*              *bi* round go

urds *gate* fo          *ju ju and ob*              *i* they fart p iss they shi                    t in the ed                         dy of time *le*

            *sang* runs we              row out to the ves                 sel you ruth

on the qu                    ay you smil                         e my l

                                            ust rode her

        then s                    he was go                         ne was no

            more we des                    troy the evi

dence but the                    dust end                         ures now he

            s got the c                    lap *me lua*

    *you no*                    *lua* to voy                         age thro

            ugh the age *sin*                    *deo* without g

od or gold s                    in or sap

            phire come be                         me it was all

*dicta* their li                    ve s they soap                         the negroes rin

            se them lance                         their bo                 ils

    then o                    il them the rap

        e of tr                         oy ro

            me & af                                    rica is eve

                                    r a story a

    s the sun set              s over goré

            e so man                                    y die they s

        ew the e                    yes shut with cat

            gut drag the se                                    a s for bo

    ne for sou                         nd for b

                        one song &              sound of bon

        e as if                         from the de

            ep a son

    g a gro                    an we have he

        re ten guinea fowl                         for sale ten

    guinea hens                    we are all *dic*

            *ta* in g

        od s story                         the pea he

                    n preens in my e

    den a ra                                    ce of rud

        e she neg

        roes for be                    ads i am

            all *âme* cu

                                    red in sin what

        reason can we

    give so rare n                    ever seen on the e

        ve of mu                                    rder i eat

sup on ha

m & b                                        read was not a sin

but a mis

take not a mis                    take but a s

in they e                    at no s                    alt to save their

soul s di                              d she die a d

our man he                              was the cap

tain up and dow                  n the deck *wa*

*le* and *sa*                    *de* run from the

field the river t                    he raft *ny*

*ame* me i be                    g you bring

the lamp ma

n let s see w                    hat we have

here *him d*

*ead oh il*                    *est mort him*                    *dead* find

the river run

*wale* ru                              n run *s*

*ade* run i dif

fer from                    the others they di

ffer from o

ther negro                    es grin gap                    e and ape ci

rce creates the s

tars god the nat

ion circe how                    ls des

troys a riot                    a circ

us of mur                    der she who cre

ates & des                    troy s is no mo                    re give us this

day our ne                    groes our profits                    *n*

*yame ny*                    *ame* we give be

er to *nya*

*me mea cul*                    *pa mea c*

*ulpa mea* we                    b of lies m

y great bla                    me and ra

in ran red fort

une flam                    es feed s our nig

ht s di

es we stand o                    n the rim the cr

ater of                    the absolute    *va*                    *nona va*

*ti revesa* do                    wn the river we f

led to the fo                    rt at the po

rt with the negroe                    s w                                    *ale* and
              *sade*                        flee dow
                        n the river                        *do not*
*read this ruth*                        *it will destroy you*                              s
              am my lad                                        jot these no
                    tes these tunes                    *fa la s*
        *o fa la m*                        *i so*                    *fa la* i
                t is not a fit j                ob for a la
    d his first ta                ste of s                in once only
                a tas                        te of mu
rder leads to a                taste *this is me*

                                    *ant only for y*
        *our eyes* ri                              *ma* all is ri
                    *ma* gin and be
    er gin and bee                                r the crew cri
                es yam wa
ter *omi*                        they flag n                    o wa
        ter yam pap *f*                    *o mi omo*
                *sade* feeds *a*
            *de* yam p                        ap what do
es this me                an *que es es*                *to* they cl
        ap and c                        lap and clap
                why th                        em not u
    s why u                s why no                    t them so
            rt the negro                es one by o
                ne all creatio
                                n mourn s this a
            ct they are pen
t up for too l                        ong *mi have mi o*
            *bi in mi tê*                            *te pot* river ti
    des drag u                        s down to the fo
            rt drag the se
        a for bodi                        es find the river we
            came from *nyam*                        e bring the la
mp men my e                            yes grow di
        m we le                    ave a tra                il a map of s
    in for all            who come a                fter the tra
        il leads *wa*            *le & sa*                *de* to the fo
            rt at the port o            n the river *ò*
*sun* cries                    *il doge* o                n his thro

160

ne the red pop

      e too b           less me p

ater for i am s         in what the ca        use loud ran

    g the sin             g and so

      ng of sang

   *le sang le*               song *le s*

  *on el s*      *on* there was a      gue so

    me fa         int piss & bi

     le there was         but me

      n must eat a      h but the p

us the pi        ss & the b

   ile sad *sad*        *e* sad sa

    d *sade* o        ne deal

led to an o      ther and ano

   ther the she      negroes sin

     g sa

d songs sing      song voi

  ces at da      wn we beg

   in they l

     imp they cry *act*    *six scene*

*ten daw*      *n wars with nig*

  *ht cir*

     *ce sage*      *and oracle i*

   *s centre stag*   *e with her wa*

*nd she sen*   *ds storms to be*

   *at us all*      *about* where e

ver the winds     throw u

   s there we plan    t a flag for nat

  ion po      pe or kin

g strum me a     tune at dawn be

   fore i di     e she     rent my re

  d cape su   ch a grand gard   en with stag

s grouse and   deer an e   den the lad la

    y dead and a    nother & anot

  her they a     ll lay d

    ead *i hate the s*    *in ruth so*

*why d*      *o i* sif

      t the ne

groes one      from the o

   ther & stru

m me a tun                              e louts all w

ho lust for a sl                    ut not i pra

            y for me ru                      th *o*

    *ra or*                        *a or*              *a* pray i s

        ay at da                      wn it be

                gins i sal

ute *il doge*                        the king in u

        s in *ius*

            pin hi                              m down her

too we ho                  ne the rag

        e of the age

    wed the wo                      e in we to *i*

                *us* yam n

            egroes we b              e we be f

    ree now they fa          ll we cag              e them was i

        t necessity hit      her hard we three

    and her pa                      ps the dog

                and her p              ups play me

        *ewe* him              *lua* she *e*

*do* we had su                      ch a time rut

        h the corn wa                      s rip

            e in the fields

    as were you mea              sure the law with c

            are not too mu              ch jus

                ice with a to

        w & a row &                      a row row ro

w we fal

                    l our lies t              ake wing so

        ar to jo                      in our ame

ns & *aves* how              did we get he

        re just u

                s ruth you and m              e in the g

    arden our ed                  en will he

            throw u                  s out as he

has be                  fore in that i

        n stance of s              in i see all

    they we          d woe to w              ant to wa

        r to water              hey ho

            ld her un          der a cloud

of nec          essity and rain                      we sa

iled so man
y man neg
roes she ne
groes yam
negroes hi
t her if she res
ists i mis
s the city
ruth y
our li
ps it grow s d
rear and sad
and we are b
ut slav
es to sin
our pi
g got go
t our pig
in a po
t the di
n of negroes
the lu
re of wa
ter and
the lu
st for war fins
find the fu
n in frenzy in s
cent of *le*
*sang* in n
egro me
at in go
re *tear this*
*up des*
*troy this a*
*ad it do not*
*fter you re*
*read it i di*
*d not writ*
*e it it i*
*s it is*
*not* not a stor
y or a tal
e to be tol
d our ne
gro our p
ig in a po
t we mis
took negr
oes for s
laves sla
ves for ne
groes i rid
e my mar
es of night
hard alm
s for the
poet of t
roy we
beg *new scene*
*il doge sno*
*res a vase of as*
*ter s and rose*
*s near*
*by* my soul
flag s some di
ve others a
re throw
n others th
row thems
elves *een hand*
*uma perna la*
*main el ma*
*no el pie u*
*n bras* a
fist an
arm a
leg a
hand a h
ead a co
ld tear ta
me this she
negro ta
ke her
arm the ro

pe men ro                    me shin

es so do        es troy in the nig           ht of my mi

nd cast th                  em o              ver a cas

e of port win                        e for y

ou my ma              n *it was a c*         *ase of m*

*urder i te*                    *ll you* in th

at insta              nce of s              in he sees al

l i tire can s              it no mo

re cl              ams feed on we

eds weeds fe              ed on fle

sh we din         e on neg

ro me              at grow fa

t the son       g calms *fa so*              *la fa s*

*o la mi m*              *i fa so*              *la* am ra

m am s         am i a              m am *âm*

*e* am ha       m h              am w

e am h         am a              m h

am *you we*         *re so wa*       *n the day i tò*

*ld you my sh*       *ip was al*              *out tò sa*

*il*dum d         um de du         m we bro

ught them to mark       et fat she

                              negroes

a bust              of our ma

d king near my b              ed i ti

re gr              ow sad *sa*

*me scene ag*         *ain il doge ga*

*pes & grin*              *s a rict*

*us* will we me

et aga              in at the sto

ne cairn with the mo       ss grip her fa       st we fast be

fore mu              rder shun the li

ght *will you sh*       *un me r*              *uth as the t*

*ruth of my wo*       *rds finds y*

*ou* i              ron for *òg*              *ún* water for *ò*

*sun sang* for *s*       *ango* i seek the sk

i       n in              kin they              the k

in in sk                    in we rend

er them in       to n

                    egroes into b

one s              and & wat

er su      ch wit he

had the ne      gro the wo

ods we hid      e & li      e on m

oss *wal*      e sade & a      *de* hide i

n the woo      ds no res

pite fro      m o      ver with her o

ver with hi      m they se

t traps fo      r *wa*      *le sad*

e & a      *de* i serve h

im they se      rve me sit

rapt at my wo      rds such an      ger pent up fo

r so lo      ng to re

st and rep      air my so

ul i d      raw near t

o thee g      od pra

y the saint s he

ar my p      lea s such a fe      at from k

in to s      kin we tra

verse the se      as let us in

vest in ne      groes a bull ma      rket bring  b

ell brin      g drum & tars

bring *do*      *n don* & go      *n gon* the op

era over we d      rop her o

ver we eat e      gg drop so

up fish ro      e & h

am *scene nev*      *er seen be*

*fore* the wo      ods drab and d

rear in win      ter the negro

es hew woo      d for fire *wale*

*sade & ad*      *e* are prey su

ch anger i ha      ve never see

n the la      d lay dead no mo

re his age we

are lat      e they are so

late for ti      me we sal

ute you my cap      tain my lie      ge lord they r

an and ra      te for *w*

n too la      se the t

*le* for *s*      *ade* & *ade* par      se the t

ruth in m      urder in s

in we are t      heir bane ene      mies to their lif

     e and we a      re of f to me

     et our fat      e their fa

te a date i da      re not mi

     ss foo      d for fi

sh for eel fea      ring the truth t      hey fret an

     d fret we eat      ham and spu

ds with port

     we rou      se the su

n with our a      cts they with t

     heir cries the po      et writes in sa

nd a pra      ise song for t

roy & r      ome for f

     ez & for the cit      y for gold tin

gis for all pla      ces at the e      nd of t

     ime & out of ti      me for *a*

*fer* the *ter*

     *ra afra* for y      ou & all that i

     s lost first we      bream the shi

p of sea we      eds be fo      re we set sa

     il they pee      r into ti

me drug of a      ll who li      ve on bo

     ard there were d      rum s & b

     ells so all co      uld dan

ce at eden the      re is bre

     am & carp in ou      r pond they fi

sh for do      ry up the run

     gs to the to      p of the ma

st lad wha      t do you s      ee *mi*

     *se en sce*      *ne il doge we*

*ars a red tog*      *a the goat ru*      *ns* so we can li

     ve in ease so      you can li

ve in great e      ase figs and or      ange s hot bu

     ns tea a se      cret ra      ce so a

lien to all we      hold dear *the*

     *n she shows u*

*s her bare a*      *rse and fall*

     *t* at night ba      t s come out t

o play how ju      st is this on

     e bag of sp      uds with grub

s the gib　　　　　es the cur　　　　　se s they cu

　　　rse us in t　　　　　heir own words

　　　　　　　　　the most fou

l words *in*　　　*da gora ri*

　　*ze mate ma*　　　　*te* who cur

se d me what　　　is this c　　　urse that i sho

　　uld be so lo　　st even the ora　　cle cur

se s u　　　s leave s us　　　to our fat

　　es at ves　　　pers we rec　　ite god ver

se s most fo　　ul words wha

　　t do we cre　　　ate he b　　　et her

　　at card s he lo　　　st her drat

that rat my　　　suit was　　　heart s him

　　　　up there gold

　　nails in his h　　　ands fe

et on his he　　　ad gold tho

　　rns save the s　　　lave in u

s in y　　　ou when the g　　ong so

　　unds s run in bet　　ween our am

　　　en s & our *a*　　*ve* mari as run i sa

y from our me　　as & culp

　　a s run for y o　　ur life run *wa*

*le* run ru　　　n *sade* r　　　un run *ad*

　　*e* run *w*　　*ale* and *sa*

*de* run fo　　r their liv　　e s *sade* ha

　　s sore tea　　ts *scene il do*　　*ge a red tog*

*a a man*　　*e of gold h*　　*air he fum*

　*es* the negro i　　s a pest to b　　e rid of him

　　up there nai　　led to woo

d to the mas　　t we slid　　e on a tide of pro

　　fit to murde　　r rob them o

f all they cr　　eate she spins a t　　op drops

　　a ston　　e into the de　　ep be co

　　me s bone *te*　　*amo te am*

*o on*　　*ly you r*　　*uth but now s*

　*he has my mi*　　*nd in de*

　　*ath* he deals t　　he cards we si

t rapt who w　　ill win her the fi　　get the to

　　re is hot

ng s & the iro　　n s she i

                              s his now
              the sun go                        es round as eve
        r how lo              ng had they la                    in there sk
              in on fi                  re rub the s
              kin with o                        il *wal*
      e and *sade* ha              ve one go                  at *agbo*
              *the ob*              a sobs ag
                      ain & a                        gain the *oba* so
        bs *oh ye ye*                  *lantic oh*                  *oh ye ye oh*
              *omi omi omi oh*              we be aro    oun *ẹbọra*              *omi oh*
*omi oh*      *omi ojú*              *ye ye lantic oh*                  *omi omi omi oh*
    *ẹyọ*              aro orun              oh ye ye oh ye ye oh
        *lantic oh*        ca ri be eh oh                  *oh omi ero*
*oh ye ye oh*        ma abo oh                  *oh mi ẹbọra*
        *ye ye lan*        *tic oh ca ri be*              eh sho ala o mi o
    o dò              o fa un              sho ca ri be              eh sho omi nla
      lan tic oh              oh ye ye oh              oh ab wa ma
              e oh ye ye oh              omi o omi ọmú              abo wa ba
*oh ye ye oh*              ma abu oh              ise ni ise ini              omi ara
        abu di ni              omi ok un              oh oh ye ye oh
*omi omi*        oh omi mí mó              a la o fa un              ma abu oh
      oh ye ye              gari be eh              oh ye ye oh mi
        sho soh a bwa              o mi abo wa ba
*oh ye ye oh*              oh lan tic oh              omi tú tù
        oh ye ye omi ara              orun omi òsun              oh ye ye o
    omi dí dùn oh              omi e lu              ju oh omi              òsà
  o              ye ye we b              e se              a kin wa
      wa              water ki              n be cam
*from omi*        *ìyè we be*        *ẹbọra àkì*              ash
        es and sa        lt for the bo        die s              of kin un
        der the sk              in of s              ea whe
re repo
        se the bo                        ne sou              ls of kin
      can y                        ou not he
ar *sub voce*              the voi                        ces *au*
      *di* of kin *a*              *udi* in the wind                  part wat
        er part bo              ne par
        t salt *le*                        *sel la sa*
                      *l salis* in *le*

*sang* sa   lt in the e   ye salt i

n the h   air salt un   der the na

ils sal   t in the e

ars sa   lt in the no   se salt on the s

kin salt un   der the sk

in of the s   ea bo   ne sal

t sk   im the sk   in of the se

a for the wo   rds the voic

es of k   in the trap   of rea

son binds u   s in the net

of time we s

kim the scu   m of prof

its they their k

in long lo   ng ago th

ere wa   s a tal

e to b   e told a to   ugh ma

n rough on a   ll the she

negroes too stern   men of ste

rn mi   en we ar

e we run our li   ves by b

ell & go   ng the ring s o

f sin gro   w ever wid

e the terns ma   ke rings abo   ve so to

o the fi   ns in the se

a we ea   t ham we e   at bre

ad we eat fi   sh fresh fro

m the deep   *w*

*ale* and *sa*   *de* e   at fr

esh fish f   rom the r

iver we b   e fresh wa

ter neg   roes the sea is *ma*

*i* is *mère* i   s *mer* is

*mar* ema   & *mater* i

s *madre* is   ma is   *omi ò*

*ab wa ma*   *e* gar

den grubs al   l over me a   m hot the he

at we are de   af to their cri

es *ba le*   *g ba l*   *eg ba*

leg b   *a leg* ba

*leg*                              *ba leg* give th

          em the se

                    a to pro                    ve to kin

  g nation & f                    lag lend your e

          ar to their cri                    es mine

      too they giv              e them                    selves li

fe we gi              ve them the li              fe of bone n

    ow the sea gi              ves up the se

          cret of bo              ne es oh

es es oh                    es *os o*                    s they ask fo

      r water we g              ive them s

    ea they as                              k for bread we

                give them se

      a they ask for lif                    e we give them o

nly the sea *was*              *that a fair*

          *trade ruth i*              *ash you i*

  *am a fair*              *man* by b              ell and go

          ng the crew              dance a re

    el on board the                    negroes play the d

                rums to the de

        ep s with them                    they sin

g as they fa              ll bles                    s me *pater*

          i am all              sin by wo

      rd and d                    eed bless him *pa*

          *ter* give him this d                    ay his b

read his wat                    er his profit s a

      bove blue oce                    an of sky

                waits cal              m no clo

ud under us bl                    ue sea the ear

      th groans it w                    as the dri

                *ve for pro*              fit *douce do*

        *uce mi amo*              *r we be i*

*bo we be sho*                    *na ban*              *tu  we b*

      *e fa*                    *nte edo & ra*

*da that da*              *y at the man*

      *se we at*                    *e were sa*

                    *ted with ve*

    *al and wine bet*              *ween us there we*

*re no wil*              *es did I du*              *pe you ther* e was on

*ly ought* we ga                    ve them go

d & gave the                    m good they gi

ve us good &            & go                    d be

ar the we                    ight of ours

ins light as the su                    n s beams there i

s shit & pi            ss bile & pu

s there is s                    in he rose will

i will he        hew a  beam of wo

od for the mas                    t strong to ha

ng them from

did I write t                    hat ham and fi

sh roe dates and fi                    gs sweet me

at s we din            e on neg

ro meat & o                    ranges a lass of t

en serve s u

s mind y our s                    tep now lad

on bread and w            ater we bree

d them ble            ss me *pat*

*er* for i have        set a snare for *wa*            *le* & *sad*

*e* a trap for h

is feet a sna

re for hers *w*            *ale* and *sade* are ti

red we grow tir                    ed more mis

fortunes than i                    can no

ink my pen ca                    n write no mo

re here            on the s

kin of the sea

how do i ge

t this to y                    ou if only i c

ould write on wa

ter my sins ha

ve the s                    ea say to yo

u what i can

not i he                    ar only the ro

ar of r

aw water t                    he sea s voi

ce a fis            t to the he                    ad if you hap

pen upon my s            in the sea gi

ves up it s d                    read secret w

ho can bear t                              o hear the bo

           nes of g                                    od lie here

scene he sin              gs a pint of a                         le & on

        e dead ne                         gro on the alt

           ar of our gre                          ed where li

   ve our *la*                    res and *pena*                    tes we ab

                                        use the ab

              solute in g                    od goo

   d & ma

                              n       for a t              roy ou

        nce of go                                ld a ba

   r of s                alt we be                              at our h

                                   eads *oh ye ye*

oh ti                        me is tard                     y late in tim

        e i lon                         g for cold lak

           es the harsh wind                        s of the dow

ns the bli                              ss of the p                    ast my hope

   traps me m                              y na

              me is you *y*                    *ou big man*

     *me i see yo*                        *u to wri*

              *te wri*                              *te a*

                        *ll ti*

   *me me wa*              le you wr                              *ite for m*

           *e* such an un              common man *me i s*

*ay you writ*              e on pap                              er i wri

        *te* de                    *ar sade you b*

*e my queen e*        *ver me i mi*                        *ss you and a*

        *de al*                *l my lif*                    *e i* a

m do              ne he ta                    ke s the pa

   per e                    ats it the                              n he fa

        ll s on his li                    ps *sa*

                   *de fé*                    *mi i*

      *fá if*                    *á if*                    *á* if o

        nly *ifá* he fa                    lls to the we

           ight & wa                    it in w

ater i ca                                        ll his na

                   me & f

        all too t                              o my on

ce my no                         nce queen of the ni

                ger the sa                                         ble o

    ne *nig*                        ra afra

            sa                                         d

                    *e oh ye ye* afr                    i

        ca oh o

                ver and o

    ver the *o*                         *ba*   s

                            o

            b

                                            s

---

Bektemba Agbeke Gholahan Fasuyi Abifarin Olurun
Fadairo Abiona Nuru Okunade Dolap Moyo
Olufunke Olupitan Falana Esi
Kobena Atoapem Kwesi
Nahe Sade
Ade

*Ebora*

seas                                                                          there is o

        this ti&meurder my lord                                                              oh  oh

oracle    within    over                my liege lord

                        my fortunedes                           time within loss

                there are   my us

        oh  oh      a sin          ora              my we

                        ora    ashes                                    video        my fate

        my god      ora    over                                        video

                        ora pro    ifa          video

                                        ifsaunder crew from

am                                        captainifa i

        ftord        this is but an oration            of loss            own from

fa          time sands the lossosithisay                        slave

        farose for Ruth                        falkldieg from

                        and              i am                      writer

                over    for truth          from

                visions                        &                      mortality

over and over                    over                    supporste truth

        the crewntomthekinga sobs            then

        no provisionsofinding a way                        there is fate

                le p'tit mort            found            there is creed

from is                        scent of mortaldiyt        there is

        to was                              a rule                      oh oh

        ought evidence   she   water parts

                        falls        the oba sobs again

fa fa fa                    suppose                        sdhrey oelhesr ssocbbss

        fatlhiecg                                        ifa ifa ifa iwith she

truth            a rose                                to            negroes

there is creed            the    port                                    man

there is saxteven                              over            negroes

                              salve the slave
        this is but an oracle *salve* to sin          s*the* *oba* sobs
*video* *who* *kinds* *this* loss within                    i am
                         am                                    and *ave*
there is creed          lord*ve*          vi*sions*              *ave*
there and *ater*              a rose i say
    a rose for Ruth here is   the *oba* sobs
        no provision *and*    oh  oh
        oracle          for truth
from is                                        suppose truth
    to was          there are          the*n* the seas
finding as *save* the yam h  oh      with she
            found              cut *the* *ghost*
        and *save* the yam  *export*
            negroes          not th*for* *heat* murder my lord
payment you *my* liege lord ought evidence      suppose  *ifa*
        then          what for   my dear *ifa* i
    *fa*                    a rose *my us*
th*e* rat   the rat      truth      my we          my fate
*my* *gods* the cat          over          falling
the cat got the rat          & sunder crew from
    over              with *captain*
        own fresh falls          &
*found* the crime          slave          over
        a rose *the crew* touching          under from
be absolute          writer          found africa   there is fate
        underfrom                         there is creed
        water          mor*tality* ear   there is proved
    justice          dang*erous*                        oh oh
do you hear *that* *the* law
        *le mort*      sound *to raise*   the *oba* sobs again
        *le p'tit mort*      s*he died*   sos sos sos      *ifa ifa ifa i*
                    the died          os
            scent of mortality          *os*    the
        seven                          I hear *a* *bell/*s
seas              *she* us *os*                      ring out
Dear Ruth          this th*at* *s*          save us *os*
    *ifa* *ifa*          salve & save
this is a tale   falling              to  our  souls      time within loss
told cold              t*urn* & turn
a yarn  a the *ones*          *ora*          over
        &      & *ora*
        over *declared* *our* *souls*
do I              my fortunes *ora pro*   us souls
have          bone souls                          water parts

dear4Lisa

Dave ask/s that i

when did we decide you     Circe the crone          these words come from his lips
though one hag seer                          my hand shapes them          she
                              the illustrating                                    sh/h
              apes all lips          of dead
sing sing same            of died                          not so loud
                    they sang        sing at once
didn't the bell ring          a sad tune          oh oh
I come from the north     le song moans          el song               my ass
              the dales sing again          moon can
land of mist                    he          ann          my goat bag
of hoar-frost          ann          ann          palm with the
          the time and date of sin          hearts they
    sow the seven seas          groan too          &&
          ffoo  with ave/s      the sin      the din      the
    with ash  din    of dying          why did we          writ in
          decide when did we the dead          decide     sand
              the died      the dead          live rent    sing i say
    i come from    my own                    my       lives
    i come from    the north          very own the
        the north   dales  the          land   hey hey ho
          dales   of mist  land                of hoar frost
        there is rust in      the time and date of hoar frost
                  of sin insure time and date
    he had an ace          of sin
                              i a sequence of
          queens          one
              king                              chu
          Sam       the rum
                        dear Ruth can a tale be
  mortality by the tail          ever
  mortality why the tail      if told
  on the run              cold                    a secret race
  mama                          *underwriters
  mai          calms       lives      of writ/s &          rent/s
              calms
          calms          the truth
          calms   to the right              to be sure
                        this is but
  writ in sand              an oration
  write in sand                      a tale
  lives life              old
  rent life       as sin          is new
    when did we decide

                        the seas
                    there is   with she
creed there is                    fate the negroes
        is oh       man      there is                    negrob soracle
creed there is lord          there are              fate there
    my liege lord              oh  oh                    oh oracle
        ashes there are            my *deus*
                    oh my plus       over
            my we   ashes   *ifa*            my fate
my god        *ifa*                    over
                    suffer crew from          *ifa i*
    *fa*            *ifa* captain                    *ifa i*
fa           own from                        *ifa i*
    *fa* fa            slave            falling
fa           over            under from
    fa            writer        fall                &
    ing of from        over
        the crew            mortality    touching there        &
    is fate            ou mort                        water parts
        the crew        there            the *oba* sobbing there creed
        is fat *de mort*            there
    *le p'tis mort* here        oh            is creed h
            there      the sobs of mortality
                is        oh            oh the *ifa ifa i*
sobs           she       again        the
    seven       falls            *ifa ifa ifa i*
seas *ifaifaifa*   over                the        *ora*
    seven   falling this time     *ora*        to
within            seas      port        *ora*
    *ora*            *ora pro* over                time
        this time within      *ora*
    this is but an    over        within        *ora*    oration
            my fortunes      time sands a loss
            with a sin        you say time        in i am
*video video video*        this is   lord                but an o
            who says ration of loss        time
    sands        i say visions        the loss        a rose
    a rose for Ruth with        over and over        in i am
            and   lord of            the *oba* sobs
        no provisions            for loss this from is            o
    ver and o        to was        suppose truth   ver
            the seas        then        the *o*            water parts
finding a way        *ba* so        with she        the *oba* sobs no pro
        found        visions from is        negroes
    to was            man            a port   sow

dear Lisa

Dave ask/s

that i          to the right                    write Clara

to be sure                    these words              the tune
to you
this come from his lips        tears      but my hand shapes air
them                          an oration      &      it calms me    sh/h
a tale      apes all                      but then the drum/s
sing      old                              & oh the drum/s sing
all night      why are we here      as                  not so loud
they sing              ask &
didn't
they pray for death the bell ring new                  where are
not le p'tit mort                    we sang
oh oh
they shout lisa le the crone      dance    el song
we act the past but lison            lisa dance
my ass lison
the facts      a/gape    hot              dance  sing again    what does it mean
sings                                      pain
Dear Ruth captain  pain                          my goat bag of
tune
can a tale                      palm wine      sad tune
they tell
be told                      they lie                          they
with no
sow the overseas                notes        groan              ma ma
Dear Ruth                                                    moi je am
with ash if a tale  a fortune in forts      he    sing am              she
a pint of gin and be told and                      him ob am
day print
sing i say    the                      him ask this is an oration heaves
like me
ora      my                  own              to                my    &  for me
ora      they sobs again    fro              groans        the din    of
everybody
ora              the candle flame/s ho                          writ in
dancing
the tale is old      when did we decide          once  the          dead        the
begins
old as sin      there is ruse                              in dis    sand
died
ii nome                              from    insure    scond lives rent life
dee                                              dies
Circe      he had an      the north              the          dies
the crone                      dale a sequence    land
the hag                as                                      of hoar frost
the seer              queens                          of mist
she of the sting      date                          one  the time
& king                                          chu
her lips gape              Sam the rum      of sin
wind strum/s the air sings a tune there is    us    dear Ruth    &
a sad tune
he strums the oud can a tale be          os
with no notes      the ship cradled      told      there is bone
why does the sting bone shine so                moi
our lust          a secret race          moi rains
it
our loss              piss          underwriters
in
all that is old  lives          &  of writ/s    am
& rent/s      in this new age      bile cede      he
the truth      ran pus      am

                                    told
*ba/ba*                    cold                                    sh/h
*iya*                                              the      have your
*ifa*                          clarion                    ear i shave me
      sounds        rave i *rev* now                    for      *je*        do you
            me            A clear draught osasis it                    hear      a detail him
      *reves*      the          no mist in the valport and an                    pass
            *les*          the dray cart      *reves* in the              the Ife was  peas
                          the bay in the cart              pleas  of
                  of mied rollop clopulip gallop            hard  slap
&            den you land der                    and i Ruth will slap
      the                          slapave stag/s            sobs oh    boar/s &
      sail the sobs    Sam    deer                        carpish & mud huts vast
                  only            mate the        the river doves                when
we will rush the huts              there                            *nbu*      if
will be dogs                  sobs  & fish    aglus            let we rush de &ap/n
            to                      seal grouse  *omi se*              this owls & crow
      tit/s pea/hen/s too for skin thud        over            pigs and        of over
hold him    negroes                &she again        sin  this
negroes *je*          lead her ed of            of  *reve* hat            greed
                  a deal          *reve* pain has        my
      elation      abliga se with *mes*  new        ran it        reeds                the
erase this            riot                that hat my      the        seal
            on  erase me    sea/s    drafen ifun man  deal  feeds              the
*ave*                  well                  lust  done                    for
*ave*                  i            see  you    tin    th Kate a sin for    gold
*ave*                      comes            clad  we will      rest
      slave                    in        in fur    rest ush the captain
            ring        save the *ave/s* rest howmy      the pet many
            cara save the *salve/s*            my    she
            negro how do      the *vale/s* too              you ask me I beg dem fo *Ayo*
but Sade the slaves          forty    we                    parse  i
*sayi omo*  Ben  the  lad    the deed is      lay      dead it one  *mi*          *omo*
fo mi *pic/kin*              or              *mi*          big crow clear with
            Ruth this    many how is a  scum for tea
bite him                  dafbe sun's rays  told        we
him big cold          an          hot        praise  old      the
him *fun/fun*            dead      the gibde      itone
      note a                is held him lesb her    a    an    job well
they ngro            aria        done      for    the  Clair
hey dpain      Kate    for              falasaya      the
hey    &        pain the Ruth                  &rat a tat for
      pain *le pain le*      *painet pan*      pant  here's and tat tat
                          panse & the    paint        row row
Dan Jon  & Will            &      it share the roar i
the arevo fiates watery        tale

found                   gin my us                 in afric?
y/our ear     a round                        rum          my faith negroes
thergo    here aster/s oh oh      od             cam fo m found africa   the mast must be teak men
       the deed   underwho can cure me       su             gain
       &                   wate            ver        for yo the cur      that that   proved
      justi      the        from                    for je ifa that hat
t           the law my liege          deep       pour ni       life  cut the cards
        days      par         *       of       under from ifa i              I won the throw
   weeks        my plea is negligent        the field her    sos   so         so        gluce
fa      mon        fro  us         i say        of wh           doge
comes fa          for   os mortafity                  aces      she smiles
cut her open  in           ssstice   star        be             b smile
   the noise        cor           suicidal   I    in lives& am              a dischange
i           ort   as th     is      oveam    save            throw falling
   le p'tit m the crew                 fssdy          Ruth                throw them
             of cell of mortality   in rations murder s       is fate crusts
but why           sum         am        tone & fine     the seer there is creed
     th  bones   she do the stars    app   nig nig   if  shine  there is under    if only
         & falls in  der m  de us          & you   where       side       oh oh
her sh   faifaifa             salve our souls the       again
   with rapt     if only ifa            nag             tense      ifa ifa ifa i
serve   round  b         is all wrongport            the the oba sobs again
and fi        men   rum ra            over  re was piss cum
seas     more rum   &               Ruth
                 thru           som or a    salve the slave    they sang &
   with          m and and    my     des         sang he     with sin  we map
      uncomm         salve   ora pro you       nigh      water/s leak        time
   vid       deo     within e a sea       le     g      put         birth
the market this       aro  nd  tim      sang     av cord  such
   th           her  i say  groan  ve        a rose i pen                     further
        a crost for Ruth fat nig   dugs here      tea       ver seer
i      go          you    re  va    lot            all lord    payment
n    God  no we were write   for     to    yo         a lace cap for my what for
you God st hear m    can          of li  on life           suppose truly the negroes with
         toys  ov                         do you hear the lute
f        lady a gold    should cut the cord of this story sound to raise oba sobs
take every th              on      fro    my case
cum gran       d    a so            is   ort       sow     in negligence
with a grain of salt  dire visions   ve         tell /s my p       night water parts
      the be       ought evidence   the             rong        necessity
th  Ruth reed  then   vedic      mu     negroes     ave t  you
th             against sur      th   a rose prom    you    to ile ife
told cold     a            s negroes    sow the sea     m     my lord
h         Chi  my liege  dum    s     tanding
h  him   s    with sos   de    Ruth  os    w  de  &
h  too us   I d  l  she f    atio          Ben     reason

# Glossary

WORDS AND PHRASES OVERHEARD ON BOARD THE *ZONG*

## Arabic

**rotl:** unit of weight or measurement

## Dutch

**bel:** bell
**bens:** thing
**geld is op:** money is spent
**hand:** hand
**ik houd van u:** I love you
**op en neer:** up and down
**tak:** arm
**tong:** tongue

## Fon

**Age:** water god
**Da:** snake god that coils around the universe and supports the earth
**Lisa:** female deity connected with the moon
**Mawu:** male deity connected with the sun

## French

**aide moi:** help me
**aile:** wing
**âme:** soul
**ange:** angel
**coeur:** heart
**eau:** water
**il est mort:** he is dead
**j'ai faim:** I'm hungry
**j'ai soif:** I'm thirsty
**je:** I
**laver:** to wash
**main:** hand
**mer:** sea
**mort:** death
**mot juste:** the just word
**père:** father
**pied:** foot
**pour moi:** for me
**rêve:** dream
**rêver:** to dream
**sang:** blood
**santé:** health
**tais toi:** be quiet

## Greek

**beta:** second letter of Greek alphabet

## Hebrew

**aleph:** first letter of alphabet

## Italian

**il doge:** the duke

## Latin

**afer:** African (male)
**afra:** African (female)
**audi:** hear or listen
**ave:** hello, good-bye
**culpa:** fault
**cum grano salis:** with a grain of salt
**deo:** god
**deus:** god
**dicta:** a saying; in law, comments that are pertinent to a case but do not have direct bearing on the outcome.
**ego:** I
**esse:** to be
**ferrum:** iron
**inter pares:** among equals
**lares and penates:** household gods
**mea:** my
**niger:** black (male)
**nigra:** black (female)
**os:** bone
**pater:** father
**ratio:** reason; in law, the short for *ratio decidendi*, the central reason for a legal decision
**sal:** salt
**salve:** hello, good-bye
**sin:** without
**sum:** I am
**te deum:** early Christian hymn of praise
**ventus:** wind
**video:** I see

## Portuguese

**belo:** beautiful
**coisa:** thing
**lindo:** beautiful
**perna:** a leg

## Spanish

**ayudame:** help me
**cosa:** thing
**mano:** hand
**para mi:** for me
**pie:** foot
**que es esto:** what is this
**son:** the song
**yo:** I

## Shona

**afa:** he/she has died
**ari:** he/she is
**asi:** but
**ave:** so that he/she can be
**bere:** hyena
**bete:** cockroach
**bodo:** no
**dare:** court
**dede:** baboon
**derere:** okra
**dura:** granary
**duri:** mortar
**ega:** alone
**enda:** go
**fini:** cruelty
**gano:** axe for fighting
**gate:** clay pot
**go:** wasp
**godo:** jealous
**gora:** baby without father; vulture
**gore:** year
**gudo:** baboon
**gura:** cut
**guti:** when it's cloudy and about to rain, overcast
**inda:** louse; go
**indiani:** who are you?
**ini:** me/I
**ipa:** give
**isa:** put into
**ishe:** god, king, creator, queen
**ita:** do
**iva:** become
**mai:** mother
**mari:** money
**mate:** spit
**na:** with/by/and
**ndega:** on my own
**ndini:** it's me
**nego:** by a wasp
**nemari:** with money
**oda:** she wants
**oga:** by him/herself

**pera:** finished
**redu:** ours
**rema:** fool
**revesa:** speak the truth
**rima:** darkness
**riva:** trap
**rize:** scorpion
**rudo:** love
**rume:** big man
**sa:** like
**sema:** revulse
**seva:** gossip
**sora:** grass
**sure:** behind
**taita:** sister
**tese:** together
**tiki:** amount of money
**toga:** on our own
**tora:** take
**ura:** womb, intestines
**uri:** you are
**vanoa:** they have seen
**vati:** they said
**vene:** owners
**vese:** all of them
**viga:** hide

## Twi

**cedis:** unit of currency in Ghana
**Nyame:** name of God

## West African Patois

**lava lava:** talk
**tiki tiki:** money

## Yoruba

**ague:** fast
**àse:** may it manifest
**aso won:** their clothes
**ba ba:** father
**ebo:** sacrifice
**ebora:** underwater spirits
**ebo orí:** sacrificial food for Orí
**Efun:** Yoruba deity

**Èsù:** Yoruba deity
**fun fun:** white
**gbo mi mu:** drink water
**Ifà:** divination
**Ilé Ifè:** capital city of Yorùbáland in Nigeria
**ilé wa:** our house
**Inle:** divine physician who is also a fisherman and hunter
**ìyá:** mother
**ìyà:** suffering, tribulation
**iye:** mother
**ju ju:** an item which is believed to have protective qualities
**ní mi ni ran:** remind me
**ní ran:** remember
**oba:** king, ruler
**ode:** hunter
**ó d àbò:** until my/your return
**ó d ola:** until tomorrow
**odù:** statements from oracle
**Ògún:** Yoruba deity of iron
**Olú:** God
**olú femi:** god loves me
**olú sèyí:** god did this
**omi:** water
**omi dídùn:** sweet water
**omi ebora:** water in which spirits reside
**omi mímó:** holy or life-giving water
**omi òkun:** ocean water
**omi osa:** water from the lagoon
**omi se oore:** water did a kind thing
**omi tútù:** cool water
**omo:** child, offspring
**omo è:** her child
**omo e:** your child
**orí:** head
**Òsun:** river goddess
**owó:** money
**owó mi:** my money
**wa àgbò:** look for the ram

# *Manifest*

**AFRICAN GROUPS & LANGUAGES**

Bantu
Edo
Ewe
Fante
Fon
Ibo
Lua
Rada
San
Shona
Twi

**ANIMALS**

ant
asp
ass
bat
bee
boar
bream
carp
cat
clam
cod
deer
dog
dory
dove
eel
fish
fowl
grouse
hare
hen
hog
lion
mare
nits
owl
pig
pup
rat
raven
sole
sow
stag
tit mouse
toad
wolf

**BODY PARTS**

arm
*bras*
cunt
ear
eye
feet
finger
fist
hand
head
heel
hip
leg
lips
*mano*
nail
nose
*ongle*
paps
*perna*
*pied*
*tak*
teat
tit
toe
*tong*
torso

**CREW**

Alf
Dan
Dave
Don
Ed
Hamz
Hans
Jesus
Jim
Jon
Mike
Ned
Peter
Piet
Roy
Sam
Ted
Tim
Tom

| Food & Drink | Nature | Women Who Wait |
|---|---|---|
| ale | asters | Ans |
| beer | bog | Clara |
| bread | cairn | Clair |
| carp | corn | Eva |
| cider | dale | Eve |
| cod | fen | Grace |
| corn | field | Mary |
| dates | garden | Miss Circe |
| éclairs | glen | Rosa |
| egg | hay | Rose |
| gin | mist | Ruth |
| ham | moss | Sue |
| herb | ocean | Tara |
| hops | peat | Um |
| jam | rose | |
| kale | sea | |
| meat | sky | |
| oranges | stone | |
| pea | stook | |
| pear | sun | |
| pie | tares | |
| port | vale | |
| rice | yew | |
| roe | | |
| rose water | | |
| rum | | |
| scone | | |
| sion (water parsley) | | |
| soup (egg drop) | | |
| spud | | |
| tea | | |
| veal | | |
| water | | |
| whey | | |
| wine | | |

*Notanda*

*There is no telling this story; it must be told:*

In 1781 a fully provisioned ship, the *Zong*,[1] captained by one Luke Collingwood, leaves the West Coast[2] of Africa with a cargo of 470 slaves and sets sail for Jamaica. As is the custom, the cargo is fully insured. Instead of the customary six to nine weeks, this fateful trip will take some four months on account of navigational errors on the part of the captain. Some of the *Zong*'s cargo is lost through illness and lack of water; many others, by order of the captain are destroyed: "Sixty negroes died for want of water . . . and forty others . . . through thirst and frenzy . . . threw themselves into the sea and were drowned; and the master and mariners . . . were obliged to throw overboard 150 other negroes."[3]

Captain Luke Collingwood is of the belief that if the African slaves on board die a natural death, the owners of the ship will have to bear the cost, but if they were "thrown alive into the sea, it would be the loss of the underwriters."[4] In other words, the massacre of the African slaves would prove to be more financially advantageous to the owners of the ship and its cargo than if the slaves were allowed to die of "natural causes."

Upon the ship's return to Liverpool, the ship's owners, the Messrs Gregson, make a claim under maritime insurance law for the destroyed cargo, which the insurers, the Messrs Gilbert, refuse to pay. The ship's owners begin legal action against their insurers to recover their loss. A jury finds the insurers liable and orders them to compensate the ship's owners for their losses — their murdered slaves. The insurers, in turn, appeal the jury's decision to the Court of King's Bench, where Lord Mansfield, the Lord Chief Justice of England presides, as he would over many of the most significant cases related to slavery.[5] The three justices, Willes, Buller, and Mansfield, agree that a new trial should be held. The report of that decision, *Gregson v. Gilbert*, the formal name of the case more colloquially known as the *Zong* case, is the text I rely on to create the poems of *Zong!* To not tell the story that must be told.

"The most grotesquely bizarre of all slave cases heard in an English court," is how James Walvin, author of *Black Ivory*, describes the *Zong* case.[6] In the long struggle in England to end the transtlantic slave trade and, eventually, slavery, the *Zong* case would prove seminal: "The line of dissent from the *Zong* case to the successful campaign for abolition of slavery was direct and unbroken, however protracted and uneven."[7] I have found no evidence that a new trial was ever held as ordered, or whether the Messrs Gregson ever received payment for their murdered slaves, and, long before the first trial had begun, the good Captain Collingwood who had strived so hard to save the ship's owners money had long since died.

It is June — June 15, 2002 to be exact, a green and wet June in Vermont. I need — I must, I decide — keep a journal on the writing of *Zong!* I have made notes all along but there is a shift: "Am going to record my thoughts and feelings about this journey," I write, "as much a journey as the one Captain Collingwood made; like him I feel time yapping at my heels — have but 3 months to deliver this ms."[8] I flirt with the idea of immersing myself in as much information as I can find about this incident involving the slave ship, *Zong*. I begin reading a novel about it, but am uncomfortable: "A novel requires too much telling," I write, "and this story must be told by not telling — there is a mystery here — the mystery of evil (mysterium iniquitatis to quote Ivan Illich)."[9] Should I keep on reading? "If what I am to do is find their stories in the report - am I not subverting that aim by reading about the event?"

I have brought two legal texts with me to Vermont, one on contracts, the other on insurance law — a branch of contract law. The boredom that comes with reading case after case is familiar and, strangely, refreshing, a diversion from going somewhere I do not wish to go. I find out what I knew before: that essentially a contract of insurance or indemnity provides that a sum of money will be paid when an event occurs which is adverse to the interests of the person who has secured insurance. But I am hunting for something — anything — to give me some bearing, since I am, metaphorically speaking, at sea, having cut myself off from the comfort and predictability of my own language — my own meaning. A sentence catches my eye: "Surely, little in the way of authority is required to support the statement of Lord Sumner in "Gaunt" that there is no 'loss' when the insured brings about the insured event by his own act."[10] Since Captain Collingwood deliberately drowned the Africans on board his ship, I reason, he cannot, therefore, claim a loss. Does this make me feel better? About the law? But a jury of his peers found otherwise; further, how can there not be a "loss" when 150 people are deliberately drowned? Collingwood was not a seasoned captain: Prior to this fateful voyage his involvement in the slave trade had been as a ship's surgeon. In this capacity, however, he would have known that maritime law in England at that time exempted insurance claims for the natural death of slaves (which itself begs the question whether the death of someone who is a slave can ever be "natural."), but held, and ominously so, that insurers were liable when slaves were killed or thrown overboard as a result of rebellions, revolts, or uprisings.

Like Captain Collingwood, I am now fully launched on a journey. Unlike the good captain, however, I do not feel fully provisioned, indeed, uncertainty is my familiar. Can I really fashion poems from this modest report of a legal case, *Gregson vs. Gilbert* ? About a story about which there is no telling?

Another green and misty morning in Vermont — I sit on a porch, stare out at the rain and think of a ship and its cargo, of the "plentifull rain . . . that continued a day or two,"[11] of thirst and frenzy. And of a story that cannot be told. I never finished reading the novel my journal reveals — I turned instead to the law: certain, objective, and predictable, it would cut through the emotions like a laser to seal off vessels oozing sadness, anger, and despair. I yield to a simple but profound curiosity — about the sea, a captain, the sailors, and a ship. About a "cargo." And the story that must tell itself.

Law and poetry both share an inexorable concern with language — the "right" use of the "right" words, phrases, or even marks of punctuation; precision of expression is the goal shared by both. In the case of the former this concern has both material and nonmaterial outcomes. A rightly worded contract, for instance, can save an individual from financial loss, or secure great financial benefits. A proper interpretation of legislation can result in an individual's physical freedom, confirmation of civil or human rights, or even death. In *Gregson v. Gilbert* the material and nonmaterial would come together in unexpected ways. An accurate interpretation of the contract of insurance, according to the owners of the *Zong*, that is, would result in great financial benefit to them: they would be paid for murdering 150 Africans. At the same time, it would mean that the deliberate drowning of 150 people was not murder, but merely the disposition of property in a time of emergency to ensure preservation of the rest of the "cargo" — a reasonable interpretation at that time given the law governing contracts of insurance. However, even if the courts had found against the owners of the *Zong* and ruled that they could not claim insurance compensation, given the law at that time, neither Captain Collingwood nor those who had helped in the massacre could be charged with murder, since what was destroyed, being property, was not capable of being murdered.[12]

> *I enter a different land, a land of language — I allow the language to lead*
> *me somewhere — don't know where, but I trust.*
> > *· water of want*
> *Everything is here I tell myself — birth, death, life — murder, the law,*
> *a microcosm — a universe.*

My intent is to use the text of the legal decision as a word store; to lock myself into this particular and peculiar discursive landscape in the belief that the story of these African men, women, and children thrown overboard in an attempt to collect insurance monies, the story that can only be told by not telling, is locked in this text. In the many silences within the Silence of the text. I would lock myself in this text in the same way men, women, and children were locked in the holds of the slave ship *Zong*.

But this is a story that can only be told by not telling, and how am I to not tell the story has to be told. I return to my notes made the year before:

> *July 12, '01*
> *The only reason why we have a record is because of insurance — a record of property*
> *criteria for selection:*

- *verbs*
- *nouns, adjectives*
- *random selection that parallels the random selection of Africans*
- *it is in the text — the challenge, it leaps out*
- *the Africans are in the text*
- *the legal report is the tomb stone which speaks*
- *limitation — haiku, sonnets*
- *the limitation here is the text itself — the language comprising the record*

*Language appears to be a given — we believe we have the freedom to choose any words we want to work with from the universe of words, but so much of what we work with is a given.*

- *madness outside of the box of order*
- *the impulse to order there all the time*
- *grammar an ordering but a violent and necessary ordering*
- *a violent but necessary ordering*
- *there are two poems — the one i want to write and the one writing itself*
- *something underneath there but which doesn't want to spell itself out — there is an underlying current not fleshed out but there all the same*

*When I start spacing out the words, there is something happening in the eye tracking the words across the page, working to pull the page and larger "meaning" together — the eye trying to order what cannot be ordered, trying to "make sense" of something, which is what it must have been like trying to understand what was happening on board the Zong — meantime there are smaller individual poems to be found in different places on the page as the lines are juxtaposed and work together.*

*July 21, '01*
*The legal text parallels a certain kind of entity — a whole, a completeness which like African life is rent and torn.*
*This time though I do the tearing — but always there is this movement towards trying to "make sense" make it "readable," "understandable."*

- *making a whole from a fragment, or, perhaps, a fragment from a whole*
- *logic from illogic*
- *rationality from irrationality*
- *find myself trying to find reason in the language that I myself have fractured and fragmented and yet being dissatisfied when the poem becomes too comprehensible*

*The ones I like best are those where the poem escapes the net of complete understanding — where the the poem is shot through with glimmers of meaning.*

*One approach was literally to cut up the text and just pick words randomly, then I would write them down but nothing seemed to yield — this was most similar to the activity of the random picking of African slaves — selected randomly then thrown together, hoping that something would come of it — that they would produce something. Owners did have an interest in them working together, like I do in having words work together. That working together only achieved through force. In my case, it is grammar which is the ordering mechanism, the mechanism of force.*

- *am interested in them not working together — resisting that order and desire or impulse to meaning*
- *my urge to make sense must be resisted*
- *have argued that there are always at least 2 poems — the one you want to write and the other that must write itself, and this work appears to be the culmination of that because am not even using my own words. Are they ever my own words, though?*

**Dramatis personae** (justices and lawyers)
*Davenport*
*Piggott*
*Heywood*
*Mansfield*
*Willes*
*Buller*
*Lee*
*Chambre*

*All the justices agree that the action of the ship owner was wrong — in law, that is,* **but not because it was murder** *— wanting to leave off articles, conjunctions, etc.*

- *not reading text for meaning, but for something else*
- *choosing verbs and nouns — criteria for selection as Africans were selected*

To not tell the tale that must be told I employ a variety of techniques:

— I white out and black out words (is there a difference?).

— I mutilate the text as the fabric of African life and the lives of these men, women and children were mutilated.

— I murder the text, literally cut it into pieces, castrating verbs, suffocating adjectives, murdering nouns, throwing articles, prepositions, conjunctions overboard, jettisoning adverbs: I separate subject from verb, verb from object — create semantic mayhem, until my hands bloodied, from so much killing and cutting, reach into the stinking, eviscerated innards, and like some seer, sangoma,[13] or prophet who, having sacrificed an animal for signs and portents of a new life, or simply life, reads the untold story that tells itself by not telling.

Very early on I develop a need to know the names of the murdered and actually call James Walvin, author of *Black Ivory*, in England to ask him if he knew how I could locate them. "Oh no," his tone is commiserative, "they didn't keep names." I don't—cannot believe this to be true, but later on, as a result of correspondence with a colleague who is researching and writing a book on the *Zong* case,[14] I receive a copy of a sales book kept by one Thomas Case, an agent in Jamaica who did business with the owners of the *Zong*. It is typical of the records kept at that time: Purchasers are identified while Africans are reduced to the stark description of "negroe man," [*sic*] "negroe woman," or, more frequently, "ditto man," "ditto woman." There is one gloss to this description: "Negroe girl (meagre)." There are many "meagre" girls, no "meagre" boys. This description leaves me shaken—I want to weep. I leave the photocopied sheet of the ledger sitting on my old typewriter for days. I cannot approach the work for several days.

The African men, women, and children on board the *Zong* were stripped of all specifity, including their names. Their financial value, however, was recorded and preserved for insurance purposes, each being valued at 30 pounds sterling.[15]

When I return to the manuscript I find I need more working space and decide to set up another desk that allows me to turn my back on my room. There is a moment of panic: Should I be looking at all the documents related to the case, such as the trial transcripts or Granville Sharp's letter to the Court of King's Bench, with a view to using the language there as well? The text of *Gregson v. Gilbert* appears so modest, so fragile, so "meagre." I "decide against it—important to keep the limitation," I write, reminding myself that the case is the tombstone, the one public marker of the murder of those Africans on board the *Zong*, locating it in a specific time and place. It is a public moment, a textual monument marking their murder and their existence, their small histories that ended so tragically.

I fight the desire to impose meaning on the words—it is so instinctive, this need to impose meaning: this is the generating impulse of, and towards, language, isn't it—to make and, therefore, to communicate, meaning? How did they—the Africans on board the *Zong*—make meaning of what was happening to them? What meaning did they make of it and how did they make it mean? This story that must be told; that can only be told by not telling.

*July 12, '02*
*Some—all the poems—need a great deal of space around them—as if there is too much cramping around them, as if they need to breathe . . .*
 *• what am I doing? Giving voice—crying out?*

- *for the first time am looking at breaking down the words themselves and pulling words out of them*
- *the words suggesting how to work with them — I look at them and certain words leap out at me, asking me to choose them; a sense at times of doing something for these hidden people, these lost kin . . . I burn incense, eyes skimming the text for phrases, words, feelings, as one would cast one's eyes over the sea looking for bodies — so much flotsam and jetsam . . .*
- *the text is whole*
- *then rent*
- *always what is going on seems to be about water*

The poems resist my attempts at meaning or coherence and, at times, I too approach the irrationality and confusion, if not madness (*madness is outside of the box of order*), of a system that could enable, encourage even, a man to drown 150 people as a way to maximize profits — the material and the nonmaterial. Or is it the immaterial? Within the boundaries established by the words and their meanings there are silences; within each silence is the poem, which is revealed only when the text is fragmented and mutilated, mirroring the fragmentation and mutilation that slavery perpetrated on Africans, their customs and ways of life.

I witness a continuation of my engagement with the idea of Silence vis-à-vis silence begun in *Looking for Livingstone*[16]: There I explored it as one would a land, becoming aware that Silence was its own language that one could read, interpret, and even speak.

*July 30, '02*

*The poems proceed slowly — feel am getting the hang of it — the style, the rhythm. Should I do a long poem in my own voice? There is a phrase that hangs around, is always there: the ancients walk within us. A Canadian sculptor, Dawn McNutt, whose work I like uses this phrase in her catalogue. It holds me — all the ancients walk within us. It's attributed to Jung but she has been unable, after much searching, to verify this.*

*Dawn, too, talks of faults and fragments in her work.*

*The poems are about language at its most fundamental in the sense of the very basic way in which children put language together when they begin to speak, building syllable on syllable — carefully — leaving off articles: Africans want water . . .*
- *a sense of having to let go*
- *the poems demand that I let go*
- *several of the poems appear to be about water — why not?*
- *I light incense each time — in memory of*
- *words need a lot of space to breathe — breathing space*
- *and what's happening is little bits of poetry appearing within the larger poem*

$\mathcal{T}$*here is no telling this story*—

In its potent ability to decree that what is is not, as in a human ceasing to be and becoming an object, a thing or chattel, the law approaches the realm of magic and religion. The conversion of human into chattel becomes an act of transubstantiation the equal of the metamorphosis of the eucharistic bread and wine into the body and blood of Christ. Like a magic wand the law erases all ties — linguistic, societal, cultural, familial, parental, and spiritual; it strips the African down to the basic common denominator of man, woman, or child, albeit sometimes meagre. Without a history, name, or culture. In life but without life. Without life in life — with a story that cannot but must be told.

"*Oath moan mutter chant . . . babble curse chortle . . . ululation*": These words would in *She Tries Her Tongue; Her Silence Softly Breaks*[17] metamorphose into intelligible speech. To chart the outline of the wound. I am reminded of Lindon Barrett's argument in *Blackness and Value* that the shout was the "principal context in which black creativity occurred."[18] In *Looking for Livingstone . . .*, the metamorphosis occurs when the lower case "silence" of the colonised becomes the fertile Silence of the Traveler, a Silence that arises from a rooting in tradition and a knowing of what the colonial script was all about. In *Zong!*, the African, transformed into a thing by the law, is re-transformed, miraculously, back into human. Through oath and through moan, through mutter, chant and babble, through babble and curse, through chortle and ululation to not-tell the story. . . .

> "*The poet is a detective and the detective a poet," writes Thomas More,*[19] *and that's what I feel like — a detective sifting the evidence, trying to remove the veil hiding the facts.*

What did, in fact, happen on the *Zong*? Can we, some two hundred years later, ever really know? Should we? These are the questionst I confront. Although presented with the "complete" text of the case, the reader does not ever know it, since the complete story does not exist. It never did. All that remains are the legal texts and documents of those who were themselves intimately connected to, and involved in, a system that permitted the murder of the Africans on board the *Zong*.

> *August 2002*
>  · *poems about language — some poems just fall — fall into place*
>  · *the muscle of a poem is in the verbs — found that when I was working on one with no verbs — couldn't do anything with it*
>  · *muscles give shape, hold it up*
>  · *some poems just seem to offer themselves up*

> · *am here at the desk I've put at the south wall — suddenly a piece of paper floats*
> *down, apparently from nowhere — it contains notes I had earlier made on the*
> *Bantu view of death and the afterlife of ancestors — those who have died but*
> *continue to work on behalf of the living*

I deeply distrust this tool I work with — language. It is a distrust rooted in certain historical events that are all of a piece with the events that took place on the *Zong*. The language in which those events took place promulgated the non-being of African peoples, and I distrust its order, which hides disorder; its logic hiding the illogic and its rationality, which is simultaneously irrational. However, if language is to do what it must do, which is communicate, these qualities — order, logic, rationality — the rules of grammar must be present. And, as it is with language, so too with the law. Exceptions to these requirements exist in religious or spiritual communication with nonhuman forces such as gods or supra-human beings, in puns, parables, and, of course, poetry. In all these instances humans push against the boundary of language by engaging in language that often is neither rational, logical, predictable or ordered. It is sometimes even noncomprehensible, as in the religious practice of speaking in tongues, which fatally subverts the very purpose of language. Poetry comes the closest to this latter type of communication — is, indeed, rooted in it — not only in pushing against the boundaries of language, but in the need for each poet to speak in his or her own tongue. So, in *She Tries Her Tongue . . .* the imperative for me was to move beyond representation of what the New World experience was — even one filtered through my own imagination and knowing, for that would have meant working entirely within the order of logic, rationality, and predictability; it would have meant ordering an experience which was disordered (and cannot ever be ordered), irrational, illogical and unpredictable; it would have meant doing a second violence, this time to the memory of an already violent experience. The disorder, illogic and irrationality of the *Zong!* poems can no more tell the story than the legal report of *Gregson v. Gilbert* masquerading as order, logic, and rationality. In their very disorder and illogic is the not-telling of the story that must be told.

> *October 4, '02*
> *Am stumped by some of the poems. Suddenly they stop being about language and I*
> *feel tired. Seems I was trying to put my own meaning on the words and that doesn't*
> *work. Have to let them offer themselves up. Have found a batch of rough ones at the*
> *back and they move but they move more towards the lyric and less towards lan-*
> *guage. Not sure why yet.*

On their surface the poems approximate language poetry; like the language poets I question the assumed transparency of language and, therefore, employ similar strategies to reveal the hidden agendas of language. In my own work, however, the strategies signpost a multifaceted critique of the European project. Language was and is integral to this project, hence the centrality of the critique of language in my work. In the present case I use the text of the legal report almost as a painter uses paint or a sculptor stone — the material with which I work being preselected and limited. Henry Moore observed that his manner of working was to remove all extraneous material to allow the figure that was "locked" in the stone to reveal itself. It is an image that has always appealed to me, although I work with words rather than stone.

Having engaged with this idea, however, I realize that in my approach to this text I have only revealed what is commonplace, although hidden: that even when we believe we have freedom to use whatever words we wish to use, that we have the entire lexicon of English, at least those of us who are Anglophone, at our disposal, and are able to express ourselves in whatever ways we wish to (all of us who live in the so-called liberal democracies, that is), much of the language we work with is already preselected and limited, by fashion, by cultural norms —by systems that shape us such as gender and race — by what's acceptable. By order, logic, and rationality. This, indeed, is also the story that cannot be told, yet must be told.

> *October 4, '02*
> *· was one poem in which I began carving words out of other words:*
> *"defend the dead" is first one*
> *carving words out of names of justices and lawyers*
> *pig*
> *man*
> *port*
> *field*
> *wood*
> *bull*

The not-telling of this particular story is in the fragmentation and mutilation of the text, forcing the eye to track across the page in an attempt to wrest meaning from words gone astray. I teeter between accepting the irrationality of the event and the fundamental human impulse to make meaning from phenomena around us. The resulting abbreviated, disjunctive, almost non-sensical style of the poems demands a corresponding effort on the part of the reader to "make sense" of an event that eludes understanding, perhaps permanently. What is "it" about? What is happening? In asking those questions there are echoes here, more than two hundred years later, of what it must have been like for those Africans on board the *Zong*. "(N)egroes want . . . sustenance preservation rest . . . want water . . . overboard."[20] In the discomfort and disturbance created by the poetic text, I am forced to make meaning from apparently disparate elements — in so doing I implicate myself. The risk — of contamination — lies in piecing together the story that cannot be told. And since we have to work to complete the events, we all become implicated in, if not contaminated by, this activity.

The irony here is that the story is locked within the text of those individuals — members of the judiciary, one of, if not *the* most powerful segment of English society — who were themselves an integral part of a system that engaged in the trade in humans. A system of laws, rules, and regulations that made possible the massacre on board the *Zong*. It is a story that cannot be told; a story that in not telling must tell itself, using the language of the only publicly extant document directly bearing on these events — a legal report that is, at best, only tangentially related to the Africans on board the *Zong*.

In simultaneously censoring the activity of the reported text while conjuring the presence of excised Africans, as well as their humanity, I become both censor and magician. As censor, I function like the law whose role is to proscribe and prescribe, deciding which aspects of the text will be removed and which remain; I replicate the censorial activity of the law, which determines which facts should or should not become evidence; what is allowed into the record and what not. The fact that Africans were human could not be allowed into the legal text. Like the law, I decide what is or is not. As magician, however, I conjure the infinite(ive) of to be of the "negroes" on board the *Zong*. This is the axis on which the text of *Zong!* turns: censor and magician; the told and the untold; the telling and the un-telling of what cannot, yet must, be told.

In the struggle to avoid imposing meaning, I confront the tension between the poem that I want to write and the poem that must write itself. While a concern with precision and accuracy in language is common to both law and poetry, the law uses language as a tool for ordering; in the instant case, however, I want poetry to disassemble the ordered, to create disorder and mayhem so as to release the story that cannot be told, but which, through not-telling, will tell itself.

*Oct. 12, '02*
  · *found these later poems a struggle — as if having to work harder to resist my meaning — more lyric . . .*

The story that cannot be told must not-tell itself in a language already contaminated, possibly irrevocably and fatally. I resist the seduction of trying to cleanse it through ordering techniques and practices, for the story must tell itself, even if it is a partial story; it must be allowed to be and not be. The half-tellings, and un-tellings force me to enter the zone of contamination to complete it; in so doing I risk being contaminated by the prescribed language of the law — by language in fact.

The basic tool in the study of law is case analysis. This process requires a careful sifting of the reported case to find the kernel of the legal principle at the heart of the decision — the *ratio decidendi* or simply the *ratio*. Having isolated that, all other opinion becomes *obiter dicta*, informally referred to as *dicta*. Which is what the Africans on board the *Zong* become — *dicta*, footnotes, related to, but not, the *ratio*.

*November 25, '03*
*Caledon, Ontario*
*I cannot say when I first conceive the idea but once it has taken hold I know that I*
*must honour it. "Defend the dead." The Africans on board the* Zong *must be named.*
*They will be ghostly footnotes floating below the text — "under water . . . a place of*
*consequence"*

> *Idea at heart of the footnotes in general is acknowledgement — someone else was*
> *here before — in* Zong! *footnote equals the footprint.*
> *Footprints of the African on board the* Zong.

On the "surface" the *ratio* of *Gregson v. Gilbert* was that "the evidence [did] not support the statement of the loss made in the declaration;"[21] in other words, given the evidence presented to the court, the ship's owners had not satisfactorily proved that they needed to "jettison their cargo," that is, murder 150 African slaves.[22] The "underwater" *ratio* appears to be that the law supercedes being, that being is not a constant in time, but can be changed by the law. The *ratio* at the heart of *Zong!*, however, is simply the story of be-ing which cannot, but must, be told. Through not-telling. And where the law attempts to extinguish be-ing, as happened for 400 years as part of the European project, be-ing trumps the law every time.

Can I? Should I? Will I? Must I? I did. "Break and Enter"[23] the text to release its anti-meaning.

*Dec. 15, 2003, Tobago*
*Letter to CB*
*"The text has exploded into a universe of words."*

> *· have given in to the impulse to fragment the words of the text — using it as a*
> *sort of grand boggle game and set to trying to find words within words. The*
> *text — the reported case — is a matrix — a mother document. I did not come to*
> *the decision easily — to break the words open. For a while I feel guilt, as if I*
> *have broken my own rules, but that is where the impulse leads — to explode*
> *the words to see what other words they may contain. I devise a dictionary with*
> *a list of each of the 'mother' words followed by the words contained in that*
> *particular word — for instance, apprehension yields hen, sion, pare and pear,*
> *to list a few possibilities. As I put the dictionary together, little dramas appear*
> *to take place in the margins of the text and so the poem continues to write it-*
> *self, giving up its stories and resulting in four subsequent movements or books*
> *— I think of these poems as the flesh — the earlier 26 poems are the bones.*
>
> > *The alphabet is the universe of language — all the sounds contained in each*
> > *alphabet of letters and each letter a fragment — of the whole*
> *· a link between the dynamic of the text containing everything and the funda-*
> *mental flaw that led to Africans being taken.*

- *women's voices surfacing in the text — which attempts to neutralize everything suddenly references to menstruation and childbirth and rape — in contrast with the absence of women in the larger Caribbean text as it's articulated at present — and then reading the Granville Sharp's letter yesterday — 24/01/04 — there is reference to women, infants and children — that slows me down — something so raw about that letter — he is so much closer in time to it and it's not neutral — he is taking a side and I am so interested in how someone can be so contrary to his age*
- *am unable to go on when he questions how many people would have understood English when the commands were given for them to jump or throw themselves overboard — cannot read on — too much for me*

It is fall 2005: I attend a talk at Hart House, University of Toronto, by a young forensic anthropologist, Clea Koff, who has written a book about working in Rwanda and Bosnia identifying the bones of the murdered.[24] It's important, she says, for bodies to be exhumed — in doing so you return dignity to the dead. What is the word for bringing bodies back from water? From a "liquid grave"?[25] Months later I do an Internet search for a word or phrase for bringing someone back from underwater that has as precise a meaning as the unearthing contained within the word exhume. I find words like resurrect and subaquatic but not "exaqua." Does this mean that unlike being interred, once you're underwater there is no retrieval — that you can never "exhumed" from water? The gravestone or tombstone marks the spot of interment, whether of ashes or the body. What marks the spot of subaquatic death? Families need proof, Koff says — they come looking for recognizable clothing and say, "I want the bones."

I, too, want the bones.

I come — albeit slowly — to the understanding that *Zong!* is hauntological; it is a work of haunting, a wake of sorts, where the spectres of the undead make themselves present. And only in not-telling can the story be told; only in the space where it's not told — literally in the margins of the text, a sort of negative space, a space not so much of non-meaning as anti-meaning.

Our entrance to the past is through memory — either oral or written. And water. In this case salt water. Sea water. And, as the ocean appears to be the same yet is constantly in motion, affected by tidal movements, so too this memory appears stationary yet is shifting always. Repetition drives the event and the memory simultaneously,[26] becoming a haunting, becoming spectral in its nature.

Haunted by "generations of skulls and spirits,"[27] I want the bones.

*November 2005 — Munich Airport*

   *While waiting to make a connection, I sit and watch the flow of people and suddenly become aware that the fragment appears more precious, more beautiful than the whole, if only for its brokenness. Perhaps, the fragment allows for the imagina-*

*tion to complete its missing aspects — we can talk, therefore, of the poetics of frag-mentation.*[28]

Re-reading *Specters of Marx* by Derrida has clarified some of my own thoughts and confirmed me in my earlier feelings that *Zong!* is a wake. It *is* a work that employs memory in the service of mourning — an act that could not be done before, as I've argued in an earlier essay about the possible and potential functions of memory.[29] Using Hamlet to interrogate the apparently defunct place and role of Marx and Marxism, Derrida asserts that we must identify the remains and localize the dead. The "work of mourning,"[30] he writes, demands clarity: that we know who the deceased is; whose grave it is; where the grave is and that the body or bodies "remain there" — *in situ*. This imperative for identification, this necessity to lay the bones to rest echo the remarks of the young forensic scientist.

I feel strongly that I need to seek "permission" to bring the stories of these murdered Africans to light — above the surface of the water — to "exaqua" them from their "liquid graves." Indeed, the stories of all the dead. And so, not knowing what this "permission" would look like or even why I feel the need, I journey to Ghana in the summer of 2006. While there I visit a traditional shrine close to one of the slave ports in the homeland of the Ewe people, and meet with the elders and the priest of the shrine. In preparation for this meeting I must dress in cloth, I am told — traditional African cloth, and so I am wrapped by an older woman from head to toe in a beautifully patterned fabric. I remember it as brown and gold. At the shrine I make the traditional offering of Schnappes to the priest and, following the example of the elders, touch my forehead to the ground, after which, and through a translator, we talk of the *Zong*. Of its presence in my life and what it means. None of my ancestors could have been among those thrown overboard, one elder offers. If that were the case, he continues, I would not be there. I am startled. I stare at him, a compact man with the face of a scholar or thinker. A man whose face I recognize — perhaps it is the kindness I see there — although I have never met him before. I have never entertained the thought that I may have had a personal connection to the *Zong*, nor have I ever sought to understand why this story has chosen me. Fundamentally, I don't think it matters, but his comment is still disconcerting. A full year later, on recounting the comment to my daughter, she responds to his comment: "Only if those who were thrown overboard left no offspring on board the *Zong*." Once again I am startled. Again not because I want or even care to link myself to the *Zong*. I am startled at how we, that old man and I, so easily forgot the "meagre" ones — the children. Also, I believe that he, not knowing the story, was unaware that only some of the African slaves were drowned. Before leaving I make an offering to the shrine and to all those lost souls on board the *Zong*.

My flight is routed through London; I plan to spend a few days there so that I can once again visit Liverpool and its Merseyside Maritime Museum in which there is a permanent exhibit on transatlantic slavery. On my way to England from Ghana via Amsterdam, high up above the earth I am suddenly aware of why I am going to Liverpool, home of the Gregsons, Gilberts, and, not to mention, the good Captain Luke Collingwood. There will be no priests to visit, no one to talk to about a ship and its cargo — a ship that had set sail from that very port. I do know, however, that I have to acknowledge the existence of those Europeans on board the *Zong*, those who like many Africans sickened and died, as well as those who were involved in the murder of the Africans, and thus in the murder of their own souls. And so, I go down to the old port in Merseyside, Liverpool. Hundreds of slave-ships would have set off from this port for what was then known as the Gold Coast of Africa, their holds filled with all manner of things — cloth, guns, beads — to trade. For people. For men, women, and children who would, in turn, be stuffed — things — in the same hold for what would for them be a one way journey to death — living or real. I go down to the water in Merseyside, Liverpool, and pour a libation of spirits for the lost souls on board the *Zong*. All the souls. The approach to the water is mossy and slippery and on my way back from pouring the spirits I fall flat on my ass. I am embarrassed, wondering if anyone has seen me fall and whether the fall means the pleasure or displeasure on the part of the Ancestors.

For the longest while the manuscript weighs heavily: having exploded the words, having scooped the stories out of the magma of the text, the work appears too long and the apparent lyric form and approach of this second part of the book — the four movements — troubles me somewhat, although I accept it. In the fall of 2006, however, having returned from Ghana, and in a farmhouse in the Ontario countryside, the poem finds its own form, its own voice: It suggests something about the relational — every word or word cluster is seeking a space directly above within which to fit itself and in so doing falls into relation with others either above, below, or laterally. This is the governing principle and adds a strongly visual quality to the work.

*Zong!* bears witness to the "resurfacing of the drowned and the oppressed"[31] and transforms the dessicated, legal report into a cacophony of voices — wails, cries, moans, and shouts that had earlier been banned from the text. I recall hearing a radio interview with Gavin Bryars, composer of *The Sinking, the Titanic*, in which he discusses the idea of sound never ceasing within water, an idea that he suggests Marconi believed, since water is a much more "sound-efficient medium"[32] than air. I have often since wondered whether the sounds of those murdered Africans continue to resound and echo underwater. In the bone beds of the sea.

Our entrance to the past is through memory. And water. It is happening always — repeating always, the repetition becoming a haunting. Do they, the sounds, the cries, the shouts of those thrown overboard from the *Zong* repeat themselves over and over until they rise from the ocean floor to resurface in *Zong!*? It is a question that haunts me. As do the "generations of skulls and spirits."[33] The spirit in the text and of the text is at work. Working against meaning, working for meaning, working in and out of meaning.

It came upon me one day that the fugue — in both meanings of the word — was a frame through which I could understand *Zong!* In the musical sense of the word, *Zong!* is a counterpointed, fugal antinarrative in which several strands are simultaneously at work. In the classic, fugal form the theme is stated then reiterated in second, third, and subsequent voices. In a similar fashion *Zong!* is a sustained repetition or reiteration of various themes, phrases and voices, albeit fragmented. Interestingly enough, one of the pieces of music that sustained the "writing" of this work was *Spem in Alium,* a forty-voice motet by Thomas Tallis employing five choirs of eight voices. Antiphonal in nature, it prefigures in its form and texture the later fugue.[34]

The fugue has, however, another darker meaning, referring to a state of amnesia in which the individual, his or her subjectivity having been destroyed, becomes alienated from him- or herself. It is a state that can be as brief as a few hours or as lengthy as several years.[35] In its erasure and forgetting of the be-ing and humanity of the Africans on board the *Zong,* the legal text of *Gregson v. Gilbert* becomes a representation of the fugal state of amnesia, serving as a mechanism for erasure and alienation. Further, in my fragmenting the text and re-writing it through *Zong!,* or rather over it, thereby essentially erasing it, the original text becomes a fugal palimpsest through which *Zong!* is allowed to heal the original text of its fugal amnesia.

Describing one of his recent installations — *Inconsolable Memories*[36] — the visual artist Stan Douglas characterizes the work as a recombinant narrative, a technique in which he loops several different narrative strands from the present, past, and future to retell a 1968 Cuban film.[37] The "video or film works repeat looped scenes in an ever-changing order, switch sound tracks from one to another and generally thwart our reflective need for linear narrative."[38] I am excited by, and recognize, the parallels with the formal ideas in *Zong!* To my mind, however, *Zong!* is not so much a recombinant narrative as a recombinant antinarrative. The story that can't ever be told.

The parallels go further: In an essay titled "Fugal Encryptions," Philip Monk, curator of *Inconsolable Memories,* argues that Douglas employs strategies that succeed in apparently "absolving" his work of "authorial intention."[39] In allowing myself to surrender to the text — silences and all — and allowing the fragmented words to speak to the stories locked in the text, I, too, have found myself "absolved" of "authorial intention." So much so that even claiming to author the text through my own name is challenged by the way the text has shaped itself. The way it "untells" itself.

One of the strongest "voices" in the *Zong!* text is that of someone who appears to be white, male, and European. Had I approached this "story" in the manner of wanting to write the story *about* the *Zong* and the events surrounding its fateful journey, I would not have chosen a white, male, European voice as one of the primary voices in this work. My "authorial intention" would have impelled me toward other voices. And for very good reason. This realization, however, presents me with a powerful example of how our language — in the wider sense of that word — is often, as I wrote earlier here, preselected for us, simply by virtue of who we understand ourselves to be, and where we allow ourselves to be placed. And, by refusing the risk of allowing ourselves to be absolved of authorial intention, we escape an understanding that we are at least one and the Other. And the Other. And the Other. That in this post post-modern world we are, indeed, multiple and "many-voiced."[40]

Monk's use of the word "absolve" is intriguing, given its connection with the idea of freeing from debt, blame, obligation, or guilt. Within the moral framework of *Zong!*, however, I find it an appropriate word in that it points to a relation and relationship, between past, present, and future generations; it speaks to a relation and relationship of debt or obligation of spirit owed by later to earlier generations. And I understand now how this, in turn, relates to the organizing principle of relationship used in *Zong!* mentioned earlier.

As the work shapes itself after my return from Africa — in the books or movements that develop after the first twenty-six poems — words rearrange themselves in odd and bizarre combinations: at times the result appears the verbal equivalent of the African American dance style "crumping,"[41] in which the body is contorted and twisted into intense positions and meanings that often appear beyond human comprehension. At times it feels as if I am getting my revenge on "this/fuck-mother motherfuckin language"[42] of the colonizer — the way the text forces you — me — to read differently, bringing chaos into the language or, perhaps more accurately, revealing the chaos that is already there.

The stories on board the *Zong* that comprise *Zong!* are jammed together — "crumped" — so that the ordering of grammar, the ordering that is the impulse of empire is subverted. Clusters of words sometimes have meaning, often do not — words are broken into and open to make non-sense or no sense at all, which, in turn, becomes a code for another submerged meaning. Words break into sound, return to their initial and originary phonic sound — grunts, plosives, labials — is this, perhaps, how language might have sounded at the beginning of time?

There are times in the final book, *Ferrum*, when I feel as if I am writing a code and, oddly enough, for the very first time since writing chose me, I feel that I *do* have a language — this language of grunt and groan, of moan and stutter — this language of pure sound fragmented and broken by history. This language of the limp and the wound. Of the fragment. And, in its fragmentation and brokenness the fragment becomes mine. Becomes me. Is me. The ultimate question on board the *Zong* is what happened? Could it be that language happened? The same letters in the same order mean different things in different languages: ague and *ague* — the first English, the second Yoruba. The former meaning bodily shaking in illness, the latter, to fast. Take a letter away and a new word in a different language is born. Add a letter and the word loses meaning. The loss of language and meaning on board the *Zong* levels everyone to a place where there is, at times, no distinction between languages — everyone, European and African alike, has reverted, it appears, to a state of pre-literacy.

*How do I read a work like this? This is the same question I faced after writing* She Tries....

One of the names that surfaces in the text of *Zong!* is Dido and along with it a cluster of images about the historical Dido and her founding the city of Carthage. A couple of years later, as I browse a bookstore in Toronto I come upon Simon Schamas' *Rough Crossings*,[43] a work about Britain, the slave trade, and the American revolution. He recounts the story of the *Zong*, but what is startling is the history he reveals about Lord Mansfield, Chief Justice of England, who, as mentioned earlier, presided at the appeal in *Gregson v. Gilbert*. His nephew, Captain John Lindsay, was a sea captain who had captured a Spanish slaving vessel and, it appears, fathered a daughter with an African woman on board that ship — the name of that child was Dido Elizabeth Belle Lindsay. Dido grew up in her great uncle's, Lord Mansfield's, home, where, it appears, she was treated as a relative, albeit one of lesser standing.[44] The well-known English painter Johan Zoffany was commissioned to paint a portrait of her and her cousin, Lady Elizabeth Murray, which is now on display at Scone Palace in Scotland. The details of the relationship between Captain Lindsay and Dido's mother are not recounted. Was she raped? Was there ever, in fact, a relationship? Why was the child brought to England and allowed to reside with Lord Mansfield? This link between a name or word that surfaced in the text and actual events is one of the most startling of serendipitous events that have "marked" the making of *Zong!*

Another was computer related: Having completed the first draft of one section I attempt to print it; the laser printer for no apparent reason prints the first two or three pages superimposed on each other — crumped, so to speak — so that the page becomes a dense landscape of text. The subsequent pages are, however, printed as they should be. With the beginning of each movement of the second part of the book — Sal, Ventus, Ratio, and Ferrum — the same thing happens. I have never been able to find a reason for it and my printer has not since done that with anything else I have written.

I now think of the poems that come after the first twenty-six as a translation of the opacity of those early poems — a translation that, like all good translations, has a life of its own. Together, *Os, Sal, Ventus, Ratio, and Ferrum*[45] comprise the movements of *Zong!*, the story that must be told that cannot be told, which in turn becomes a metaphor for slavery — *the* story that simultaneously cannot be told, must be told, and will never be told.

The descendants of that experience appear creatures of the word, apparently brought into ontological being by fiat and by law. The law it was that said we were. Or were not. The fundamental resistance to this, whether or not it was being manifested in the many, many instances of insurrection, was the belief and knowledge that we — the creatures of fiat and law — always knew we existed *outside* of the law — that law — and that our be-ing was prior in time to fiat, law and word. Which converted us to property: *"pig port field wood bull negroe."* It is a painful irony that today so many of us continue to live, albeit in an entirely different way, either outside of the law, or literally imprisoned within it. Unable to not-tell the story that must be told.

The continued exclusion of African Americans (I would say New World Africans) from systems of value, Lindon Barrett argues, creates a need to "pursue novel or original access to meaning, voice, value and authority."[46] In its cacophanous representation of the babel that was the *Zong, Zong!* attempts and tempts just such access to meaning.

Many is the time in the writing of this essay when my fingers would hit an S rather than a Z in typing *Zong*. Song and Zong: with the exception of one letter the two words are identical; if said quickly enough they sound the same. In the title poem of *She Tries . . .* I write:

> *When silence is*
> *Abdication of word  tongue and lip*
> *Ashes of once in what was*
> *. . . Silence*
> *Song  Word  Speech*
> *Might I . . . like Philomela . . . sing*
> > > *continue*
> > > > *over*
> > > > > *into*
> *. . . pure utterance*[47]

Why the exclamation mark after *Zong!* ? *Zong!* is chant! Shout! And ululation! *Zong!* is moan! Mutter! Howl! And shriek! *Zong!* is "pure utterance." *Zong!* is Song! And Song is what has kept the soul of the African intact when they "want(ed) water . . . sustenance . . . preservation."[48] *Zong!* is the Song of the untold story; it cannot be told yet must be told, but only through its un-telling.

# NOTES

1. The name of the ship was the *Zorg*, meaning "care" in Dutch. An error was made when the name was repainted.

2. The ship left from the island of São Tomé off the coast of Gabon.

3. *Gregson v. Gilbert*, 3 Dougl. 233. The case mentions 150 slaves killed. James Walvin in *Black Ivory*, 131, others 130 and 132. The exact number of African slaves murdered remains a slippery signifier of what was undoubtedly a massacre.

4. *Substance of the Debate on a Resolution for Abolishing the Slave Trade*, London, 1806, pp. 178–9.

5. The most famous of these cases, the Somerset case, established the precedent that no one could be captured in England and taken away to be sold. Despite the best efforts of Lord Mansfield to avoid proclaiming that slavery was illegal in England, the case was quickly interpreted as establishing the law that slavery could not exist in England.

6. James Walvin, *Black Ivory*, Harper Collins Publishers, London, England, 1992, p. 16.

7. Walvin, p. 19

8. One of the early drafts of the manuscript.

9. Ivan Illich, "The Corruption of Christianity, *Ideas*, CBC Radio One.

10. Bradley Crawford, Marvin G. Baer, Robert T. Donald, and James A. Rendall, eds., *Cases on the Canadian Law of Insurance*, The Carswell Company Ltd, Toronto, Canada, 1971, p. 391.

11. See earlier: *Gregson v. Gilbert*.

12. The abolitionist Granville Sharp did try, unsuccessfully, to get murder charges laid against those involved in the massacre.

13. *Sangoma* is a Zulu word meaning healer of both physical and spiritual ailments.

14. Ian Baucom, *Specters of the Atlantic*, Duke University Press, Durham, North Carolina, 2005.

15. Granville Sharp, *Memoirs of Granville Sharp*, Prince Hoare, ed., (Henry Colburn and Co., London, 1820), pp. 242–244. In his letter to Lords of the Admiralty Sharp challenged the sum of 30 pounds sterling, since women and children were assigned a lesser value.

16. *Looking for Livingstone: An Odyssey of Silence*, Mercury Publishers, Toronto, 1991.

17. M. NourbeSe Philip, *She Tries Her Tongue; Her Silence Softly Breaks*, Poui Publications, Toronto, Ontario, 2006.

18. Lindon Barrett, *Blackness and Value*, Cambridge University Press, Cambridge, England, 1999.

19. Thomas More, *Original Mind*, HarperCollins Publisher, New York, 2000.

20. Excerpts from *Zong!*

21. See earlier: *Gregson v. Gilbert*.

22. There was evidence, for instance, that the captain had not attempted to ration the water they had on board before deciding to drown the Africans on board.

23. A charge under the Criminal Code of Canada.

24. Clea Koff, *The Bone Woman*, Alfred A. Knopf Canada, Toronto, 2004.

25. Elicia Brown Lathon, Ph.D. dissertation, *I Cried Out and None but Jesus Heard*, Louisiana State University and Agricultural and Mechanical College, 2005.

26. The events surrounding the *Zong* have long been the focus of artistic attention. The English painter J. M. W. Turner's 1840 painting, *Slavers throwing overboard the dead and the dying, Typhon* [sic] *Coming On*, was inspired by the event; so too was the novel *Feeding the Ghosts* by British Guyanese poet and novelist Fred D'Aguiar, Ecco, Hopewell, N. J., 1999. Marina Warner has also explored this event in an online essay titled "Indigo, Mapping the Waters." Ian Baucom argues in *Specters of the Atlantic* that the continued witnessing of the *Zong* atrocity by writers and artists points to an "order of historical time" that does not so much pass as "accumulate" p. 305.

27. Jacques Derrida, *Specters of Marx*, Routledge, New York, U.S.A., 1991, p. 9.

28. "Fugues and Fragments" in the online journal *Anthurium*, vol. 3, no. 2, Fall 2005. http://scholar.library.miami.edu/anthurium/volume_3/issue_2/philip-fugues.htm.

29. M. NourbeSe Philip, In the Matter of Memory . . . , *Fertile Ground: Memories & Visions*, Kalamuya Salaam and Kysha N. Brown, eds., Runngate Press, New Orleans, 1996.

30. Derrida, p. 9.

31. Poet Maureen Harris in talk at Influency, Continuing Ed., University of Toronto, December 2006.

32. Gavin Bryars, *The Sinking, The Titanic* (CD), Polygram Group, Markham, Canada, 1994.

33. Derrida, p. 9.

34. There were certain pieces of music I played often, at times obsessively, that seemed to accompany this work. Oddly enough, Van Morrison's *Endless Days of Summer* conveyed a sense of loss of something brief, beautiful, and fleeting. So did Ali Farka Toure's *Hawa Dolo*. The simplicity and lyricism of the songs of Kenyan Luo musician Ayub Ogada recalled a memory of what might have been lost to those on board the *Zong*.

35. The Southern writer Walker Percy has explored this state in many of his novels. *Percyscapes* (Louisiana State University Press, Baton Rouge, 1999) by Robert W. Rudnicki is a helpful exploration and analysis of how the condition has been treated in literature. He includes Ralph Ellison's *Invisible Man* among novels dealing with this state.

36. Stan Douglas, *Inconsolable Memories*, York University, Toronto, June 2006.

37. *Memorias del Subdesarrollo* [*Memories of Underdevelopment*], Tomás Gutiérrez Alea, director, Cuba, 97 mins., 1968.

38. "Stan Douglas," Kevin Temple, NOW, April 13–19, 2006, vol. 25, no. 33. http://www.nowtoronto.com/issues/2006-0413/cover_story.php.

39. Cindy Richmond and Scott Watson, eds., *Inconsolable Memories: Stan Douglas*, Joslyn Art Museum, Omaha, Nebr. and the Morris and Helen Belkin Art Gallery, Vancouver, British Columbia, 2005.

40. "She the many-voiced one of one voice," from "And Over Every Land and Sea" from *She Tries Her Tongue*, p. 10.

41. Crumping originated in the inner city areas of Los Angeles. It is a visceral, explosive, and expressive type of dance style that incorporates tribal and hip hop styles.

42. From "Testimony Stoops to Mother Tongue," *She Tries Her Tongue*, p. 53.

43. Simon Schamas, *Rough Crossings*, Viking Canada, Toronto, 2005.

44. Dido resided with Lord Mansfield and his wife from the age of five at his residence where it appears she was raised as a lady within the family, albeit one of lesser status. It is unknown what, if any, impact Lord Mansfield's intimate contact with his mixed-race niece may have had on his views of slavery.

45. I chose Latin to emphasize the connection with the law, which is steeped in Latin expressions, and, also to reference the fact that Latin was the father tongue in Europe.

46. Barrett, p. 81.

47. *She Tries Her Tongue*, p. 98.

48. Excerpted from *Zong!*

# Gregson v. Gilbert

GREGSON *v.* GILBERT. Thursday, 22d May, 1783. Where the captain of a slaveship mistook Hisaniola for Jamaica, whereby the voyage being retarded, and the water falling short, several of the slaves died for want of water, and others were thrown overboard, it was held that these facts did not support a statement in the declaration, that by the perils of the seas, and contrary winds and currents, the ship was retarded in her voyage, and by reason thereof so much of the water on board was spent, that some of the negroes died for want of sustenance, and others were thrown overboard for the preservation of the rest.

This was an action on a policy of insurance, to recover the value of certain slaves thrown overboard for want of water. The declaration stated, that by the perils of the seas, and contrary currents and other misfortunes, the ship was rendered foul and leaky, and was retarded in her voyage; and, by reason thereof, so much of the water on board the said ship, for her said voyage, was spent on board the said ship: that before her arrival at Jamaica, to wit, on, &c. a sufficient quantity of water did not remain on board the said ship for preserving the lives of the master and mariners belonging to the said ship, and of the negro slaves on board, for the residue of the said voyage; by reason whereof, during the said voyage, and before the arrival of the said ship at Jamaica — to wit, on, &c. and on divers days between that day and the arrival of the said ship at Jamaica — sixty negroes died for want of water for sustenance; and forty others, for want of water for sustenance, and through thirst and frenzy thereby occasioned, threw themselves into the sea and were drowned; and the master and mariners, for the preservation of their own lives, and the lives of the rest of the negroes, which for want of water they could not otherwise preserve, were obliged to throw overboard 150 other negroes. The facts, at the trial, appeared to be, that the ship on board of which the negroes who were the subject of this policy were, on her voyage from the coast of Guinea to Jamaica, by mistake got to leeward of that island, by mistaking it for Hispaniola, which induced the captain to bear away to leeward of it, and brought the vessel to one day's water before the mistake was discovered, when they were a month's voyage from the island, against winds and currents, in consequence of which the negroes were thrown [233] overboard. A verdict having been found for the plaintiff, a rule for a new trial was obtained on the grounds that a sufficient necessity did not exist for throwing the negroes overboard, and also that the loss was not within the terms of the policy.

Davenport, Pigott, and Heywood, in support of the rule. — There appeared in evidence no sufficient necessity to justify the captain and crew in throwing the negroes overboard. The last necessity only could authorize such a measure; and it appears, that at the time when the first slaves were thrown overboard, there were three butts of good water, and two and a half of sour water, on board. At this time, therefore, there was only an apprehended necessity, which was not sufficient. Soon afterwards the rains came on, which furnished water for eleven days, notwithstanding which more of the negroes were thrown overboard. At all events the loss arose not from the perils of the seas, but from the negligence or ignorance of the captain, for which the owners, and not the insurers, are liable. The ship sailed from Africa without sufficient water, for the casks were found to be less than was supposed. She passed Tobago without touching, though she might have made that and other islands. The declaration states, that by perils of the seas, and contrary currents and other misfortunes, the ship was rendered foul and leaky, and was retarded in her voyage; but no evidence was given that the perils of the seas reduced them to this necessity. The truth was, that finding they should have a bad market for their slaves, they took these means of transferring the loss from the owners to the underwriters. Many instances have occurred of slaves dying for want of provisions, but no attempt was ever made to bring such a loss within the policy. There is no instance in which the mortality of slaves falls upon the underwriters, except in the cases of perils of the seas and of enemies.

Lee, S.-G., and Chambre, contra.— It has been decided, whether wisely or unwisely is not now the question, that a portion of our fellow-creatures may become the subject of property. This, therefore, was a throwing overboard of goods, and of part to save the residue. The question is, first, whether any necessity existed for that act. The voyage was eighteen weeks instead of six, and that in consequence of contrary winds and calms. It was impossible to regain the island of Jamaica in less than three weeks; but it is said that [234] other islands might have been reached. This is said from the maps, and is contradicted by the evidence. It is also said that a supply of water might have been obtained at Tobago; but at that place there was sufficient for the voyage to Jamaica if the subsequent mistake had not occurred. With regard to that mistake, it appeared that the currents were stronger than usual. The apprehension of necessity under which the first negroes were thrown overboard was justified by the result. The crew themselves suffered so severely, that seven out of seventeen died after their arrival at Jamaica. There was no evidence, as stated on the other side, of any negroes being thrown overboard after the rains. Nor was it the fact that the slaves were destroyed in order to throw the loss on the underwriters. Forty or fifty of the negroes were suffered to die, and thirty were lying dead when the vessel arrived at Jamaica. But another ground has been taken, and it is said that this is not a loss within the policy. It is stated in the declaration that the ship was retarded by perils of the seas, and contrary winds and currents, and other misfortunes, &c. whereby the negroes died for want of sustenance, &c. Every particular circumstance of this averment need not be proved. In an indictment for murder it is not necessary to prove each particular circumstance. Here it sufficiently appears that the loss was primarily caused by the perils of the seas.

Lord Mansfield. — This is a very uncommon case, and deserves a reconsideration. There is great weight in the objection, that the evidence does not suppost the statement of the loss made in the declaration. There is no evidence of the ship being foul and leaky, and that certainly was not the cause of the delay. There is weight, also, in the circumstance of the throwing overboard of the negroes after the rain (if the fact be so), for which, upon the evidence, there appears to have been no necessity. There should, on the ground of reconsideration only, be a new trial, on the payment of costs.

Willes, Justice, of the same opinion.

Buller, Justice.— The cause of the delay, as proved, is not the same as that stated in the declaration. The argument drawn from the law respecting indictments for murder does not apply. There the substance of the indictment is proved, though the instrument with which the crime was effected be different from that laid. It would be dangerous [235] to suffer the plaintiff to recover on a peril not stated in the declaration, because it would not appear on the record not to have been within the policy, and the defendant would have no remedy. Suppose the law clear, that a loss happening by the negligence of the captain does not discharge the underwriters, yet upon this declaration the defendant could not raise that point.

Rule absolute on payment of costs.

M. NourbeSe Philip is a poet, writer, and lawyer whose previous collections of poetry include *She Tries Her Tongue; Her Silence Softly Breaks*. Born in Tobago, she now resides in Toronto, Ontario.